MW00929855

SAILORS AND HOMOSEXUALITY

From Ancient Argo to Don't Ask/Don't Tell

The cover picture is from Fassbinder's film of the Jean Genet book *Querelle de Brest*. Brad Davis appears as a sailor before what's called a *bitte d'amarrage* in French (mooring post/bollard in English), a name boys like using among themselves but avoid before girls (unless they want to titillate the maidens) because it's the most vulgar term in French for a guy's dick.

The numerous pictures have one purpose: the pleasure of the eyes.

© 2016

The inspiration of my books dates from the French Revolution with its Declaration of the Rights of Man in 1789, the end of homophobia in 1791, followed by the right of each man to marry the boy of his choice in 2013, the whole confirmed, in the States, by the American Supreme Court. My books include: *Cellini, Caravaggio, Cesare Borgia, Renaissance Murders, TROY, Argo, Greek Homosexuality, Roman Homosexuality, Renaissance Homosexuality, Alcibiades the Schoolboy, RENT BOYS, Henry III, Louis XIII, Buckingham, Homoerotic Art (in full color), Sailors and Homosexuality, The Essence of Being Gay, John (Jack) Nicholson, THE SACRED BAND, Prussian Homosexuality, Gay Genius, SPARTA* and *Boarding School Homosexuality*. I live in the South of France.
(http://www.amazon.com/author/mbhone)

DEDICATION

This book is dedicated to King James I of England who, in 1617, proclaimed: ''I, James, am neither a god nor an angel, but a man like any other. Therefore I act like a man, and confess to loving those dear to me more than other men. You may be sure that I love the Duke of Buckingham more than anyone else. I wish to speak in my own behalf and not to have it thought to be a defect, for Jesus Christ did the same and therefore I cannot be blamed. Christ had his John, and I have my George.''

CONTENTS

INTRODUCTION

Nothing in homoerotic fantasy exceeds the union of men and boys on ships, often situational, where there is no other form of relief except solitary. Sex was just as often omnisexual, as will be seen in the first section of this book dedicated to the *Argo*, a vessel of lovers happy to share themselves onboard and on the beaches they pulled onto for the night, at times in the company of women who hungered for lusty males. At the high point of British naval power homeless boys were welcome on ships as servants and help, and each had learned in advance, from other lads, what would be expected of them. Sexual liberty on the open seas was especially prevalent during the reign of James I, he who announced before his Council his love of a boy, the reason this book is dedicated to him. Pirates took their loves so seriously that indivisible couples formed, and in one documented case a captured female was caste overboard as useless in the fulfillment of the men's needs. One French captain sought out youths that he married to older salts, thusly ensuring the protection of the boys and the twilight years of the men.

Boys who protested walked the plank, and in our own times, as the reader will see, boys are also done away with, one of whom was recently stomped to death with such violence that his family recognized him only by a tattoo. Whereas Magellan garroted a man too frisky with cabin boys, today's homophobic murderers may be sentenced to life by a naval court, but the sentences come up for review yearly, meaning they can be freed at any time. A sailor on the *USS Belleau Wood* signed his death warrant by sending out a message to other ships, "2-Q-T-2-B-S-T-R-8" (too cute to be straight), while on the other end of the spectrum a Navy SEAL married his lover, and it is no longer unheard of for a debarking officer to be met on shore with an intimate kiss from his male mate.

Real Marines star in gay porn flicks and two of Hollywood's vintage actors, Hudson and Hunter, had been real-life sailors. A sublime opera, the homoerotic *Billy Budd*, was created by Benjamin Britten, the wide-screen version produced by Peter Ustinov and starred Terence Stamp. Genet gained immortality through his book *Querrel de Brest,* as did the film version's homosexual hero Brad Davis, in Fassbinder's final opus before his overdose.

I'm a boy of my times, one who prefers vocable like cock to weenie, fuck to liaison. This will be crude and offensive to some readers, but one has to be true to oneself, and today's liberties are to be cherished, even if those liberties have strict limits: a boy today would need undaunted courage to admit to his locker-room buddies that he prefers them to the chirping maidens in the showers next door.

For purists: I use numerals when I think a number is important-- especially age milestones--because they stand out more clearly, no matter how big or small the number. And please forgive my personal interventions during the telling of the lives of these extraordinary men; I try to keep them to a minimum.

ARGO
A Ship of Warrior Lovers

The Greeks considered male-male relations as normal as boys pissing side-by-side. Boys had seen differing forms and variations of the sex act long before they could themselves ejaculate, and it was possible that they had had lovers even before their puberty. To delay the inevitable laws were enacted, like those in Athens forbidding adults 18 and over to frequent boys and youths while they worked out in the palaestra, and gymnasiums and schools were closed before the setting of the sun and not open until sunrise. Fathers had to be especially careful to watch over his adult friends, often in too-friendly contact with their sons. Boys were encouraged to choose a lover after puberty, a man of 18 or so who would continue the boy's instruction in the 3Rs, would escort him to the Agora where the boy would learn from other men's discourses and interactions. In Crete the boy was kidnapped for two months with his father's consent and under the watchful eyes of his friends, two months of full sexual intercourse interspersed with continued learning, notably in weaponry and warfare and military strategy. He would learn the finer points of the hunt, a boy's passion, as well as sword, spear and archery techniques, followed by a banquet uniting his lover with the boy's friends, where the boy would be presented with gifts--a cup, a sword, perhaps armor, a cloak, a chiton, all depending on the lover's wealth and how much he appreciated the boy. The boy would then relate his two months, which could go from star-studded wonder to accusations that he had been mistreated and would therefore keep the gifts in compensation, as well as breaking with the man. The success of the boy in finding a good, well-connected and rich lover enhanced his father's reputation and was crucial in the boy's climb up the ladder of social success. The father had once been a belovèd who had in his turn become a lover, as his son would, and so on for eternity (who could have foreseen, at the hallowed time, the stultifying effects of later religions, the heinous insults and burning at the stake, and the Nazi extermination camps of the future?)

The boys were omnisexual, and girls were an alternative form of sex, a form the boys appreciated, as you'll see in the story of the Argonauts, when it presented itself. Boys and men had common interests while girls were uneducated household servants, first at the beck and call of their fathers, later servants to their husbands. The advantage of women was providing male immortality through a man's sons, wealth through the girl's dowry and property, and a clean home and decent table. The advantages of sex between males was the incredible excitation of male lust, equally shared and equally stimulating (few males were [and are] accused of making love like the proverbial ironing board). Banquets were stag affairs. They started in the late afternoons and went on into the early morning hours. The subjects were philosophical, but as the night advanced and more and more wine was consumed, conversation turned to rumor and gossip, increasingly ribald, until they became orgies, often with paid women under Pericles, often between males under Philip II and his son Alexander, especially wild among the Macedonians who did not always mix their wine with water like the Athenians. In Alexander's debaucheries women could be involved, as could men and boys during Pericles'. There was simply no opprobrium of any sort because all forms of love were deemed natural, notably under the influence of Dionysus. Of importance only was that men did the pitching, the young servers and boy cupbearers the receiving.

There was no better example of how males lived, and the omnisexuality of their lives, than on the *Argo*, a ship of lovers and belovèds, the reason why it will fill an important part of this book.

The story of the *Argo* originates with Pelias King of Iolcus whom the Delphic Oracle said would be overthrown by the descendant of his half-brother Aeson, a boy who would one day present himself before Pelias wearing but one sandal. So when Aeson had a son, Pelias set out to kill the boy but found the baby surrounded by his mother and her maidens, all weeping as the child had been stillborn. When Pelias left, the boy's mother, Alcimede, had him brought out from hiding and sent to be raised by the Centaur Cheiron. Now, Cheiron was the King of the Centaurs and the boy sent to him was not the most imminent of the boys Cheiron cared for, for among his charges had been the great Achilles who learned military science and Asclepius whom Cheiron had taught the art of healing.

Pelias had incurred Hera's wrath a first time when he killed Sidero who had taken shelter in Hera's temple, where Pelias ran her through with his sword. This was because Sidero had been the stepmother of Tyro, Pelias' mother, whom she had treated very shabbily. Tyro would later remarry and bear Aeson, who would father Jason, the boy with one sandal who now presented himself in front of Pelias. Jason had lost the other sandal when fording the river Anaurus. Always the most obliging of lads, Jason had taken pity on an old hag who needed to be carried piggyback across the waters. This was Hera in disguise who, in the middle of the stream, made herself so heavy that Jason became temporarily bogged down in mud, losing a sandal, Hera's contribution to the fulfillment of the Oracle, and her way of wrecking vengeance on Pelias.

Jason by Bertel Thorvaldsen

Earlier Pelias had come across Jason in the market place, first noticing how handsome the stranger was, then attracted to the sandalless foot which made Jason hobble. When Pelias asked the boy who he was, Jason revealed his identity. Pelias informed him of the Oracle and asked him what he would do in Pelias' place. Jason immediately answered that he would send the lad named in the Oracle to Colchis to fetch the Golden Fleece. This remarkable answer had been placed in Jason's mouth by Hera herself.

The answer struck a bell with Pelias because generations before a ram had been sacrificed and its golden fleece preserved. The story is this: There lived in Boeotia a handsome youth named Phrixus whom his aunt, when he spurned her advances, accused of raping her. The Boeotians believed this and ordered his sacrifice. The boy was taken to the top of a mountain but just as the knife was placed to his throat, Heracles, just passing through and attracted by the group of men, stayed the executioner's hand at the last moment, claiming that his father Zeus despised killing of any sort. Hermes, Zeus' favorite son and protector of boys, was ordered by Zeus to send a ram to take Phrixus to safety in the land of Colchis, where Helios stabled his white horses and golden chariot, a blessed land of pastures and islands.

Phrixus leaped onto its back but before flying off Phrixus' sister Helle begged to accompany him as her brother was her first love. Alas, flying above a narrow arm of the sea below, overcome by the vertigo of the heavenly heights, she fell from the ram and plunged into what is today called the Hellespont. Upon landing in Colchis, Phrixus sacrificed the ram to Zeus and Hermes in thanks for his being rescued. Now, the king of Colchis was Aeetes, son of the aforementioned Helios. Finding Phrixus comely, Aeetes offered him his daughter Chalciope. She in turn gave him four sons, all of whom became Argonauts, of which one was Argus who built the ship eventually named after him. The ram's fleece was placed in a sacred grove, protected by a never-sleeping dragon. Aeetes was also the father of Medea, about whom we'll have much more later.

Phrixus trying to save his sister Helle.

The Oracle of Delphi now declared that the town of Iolcus would know prosperity only when the ram's Golden Fleece was brought back. King Pelias promised Jason that when this was accomplished he would turn over the kingdom to him. But as the fleece was protected by a dragon, it was suggested that Jason accompany himself by the most valiant men alive in Hellas. Naturally, Pelias set all of this in motion because he felt that the young and inexperienced Jason would perish during the endeavor.

It's true that Jason was young and inexperienced but he received a tremendous hand in the presence of Heracles who was again passing by. Now, no one in the ancient world had had more boys than Heracles, many of whom were members of the *Argo* team. As his exploits were known to one and all, he was voted expedition leader. He declined the offer in favor of Jason because the expedition was his idea. No one had known more boys, as I've said, but this didn't mean that Heracles was a poof. To the contrary: While passing through Thebes he slept, during a single night, with the forty-nine virgin daughters of the same father. The fiftieth daughter refused him and in anger he sentenced her to remain a virgin until the end of her life, every girl's nightmare. One of his loves was a splendid lad, a shepherd, Molorchos, who had lost his dad to a lion. He asked Heracles to give him a hand in killing it but when Heracles balked, the boy said that if he didn't do what he asked in thirty days, he would sacrifice himself on the altar of Zeus. The lad himself was no tyro to boy-love, and made it clear to the hero what his reward would be if, at the end of the same period, Heracles returned alive and lusty, after disposing of the lion, ready to play night games. Like Apollo, Heracles preferred happy-go-lucky kids because they never asked for anything in return for a few minutes under Heracles' iron-strong body, a far cry from women one always had to pay, like the theater, to enter. Heracles managed to club the animal to death and then, admiring its pelt, decided it would be perfect to clothe him. But the fur couldn't be cut with any instrument Heracles used against it. Molorchos, now by his side, suggested that Heracles use the lion's own claws to skin the animal, which was exactly what Heracles did. He threw the pelt over his shoulder and was never without it from then on.

Heracles killing the Nemean Lion with his reward,
Molorchos, waiting in the background.

That's what he was wearing when he joined the Argonauts and came upon Hylas who was a crewmember. As Theocritus wrote, ''Brave Hylas, in the flower of youth, went aboard the *Argo*, to carry Jason's arrows and guard his bow.'' Soon he would be Heracles' squire, carrying Heracles' bow and arrows. It was their second meeting and all the men agreed that they formed the perfect couple, Heracles muscle bound and deeply tanned, Hylas slim waisted and light skinned. During their first meeting, when Hylas was just a kid, Heracles killed his father when he objected to Heracles slaughtering one of his bulls. This was a pitiful reason for murder, but Heracles was never known for his subtlety. For example, even in his youth he went whole hog: The poet informs us that Laomedon, king of Troy, had upset Poseidon who sent a snakelike monster to destroy the Trojans. Laomedon sent an embassy to the Oracle at Delphi to find out how the Trojans could protect their citizens. The Oracle instructed the king to sacrifice his daughter Hesione. In this way, promised the Oracle, Poseidon would be appeased.

Laomedon complied. Hesione was tied to a boulder overlooking the sea while the Trojans retreated into the safety of the walls. Among them, however, was a foreigner, Heracles, who offered to save Laomedon's daughter and destroy the sea monster if Laomedon would give him Hesione in marriage. The king agreed.

With sword in hand, Heracles was waiting when the beast slithered out of the Hellespont's gray, eddy-wracked waters onto the sandy beach where Hesione was bound like Prometheus. Heracles slew the tentacled creature and cut Hesione free. She was taken in hand by her chirping maidens while Heracles, his chest bloated with self-importance, sought a meeting with the king. But instead, the palace guard led him out of the country and told him that if he returned it would be under pain of death.

Heracles did return, however, this time with his lover Telamon, king of Salamis, and a great army. Catching the Trojans unaware, they rushed through Troy's open gates and sacked the city, killing Laomedon and all his sons except the youngest, Prince Priam. Priam as only eight when he met Heracles coming from his father's throne room, Laomedon's decapitated head held by the hair in one hand, his blood still wet on Heracles' sword held in the other. Understanding the fate awaiting him, the child tried to placate Heracles' anger by offering to make him king of Troy.

The lusty Heracles broke into laughter. He awarded the crown to the child for his levelheadedness, and gave Hesione to Telamon for his wife. He stripped Troy of all gold and silver, took enough Trojan women to satisfy his soldiers, and returned to Greece.

Heracles' mother was the virgin Alcmene who refused to lie with her new husband Amphitryon until he killed those responsible for the deaths of her eight brothers. While Amphitryon was away doing so, Zeus decided to take her virginity, as there is no source of greater pleasure than the tight sheath of a virgin. Taking the form of her husband, he declared that he had avenged her brothers and now claimed his reward. But Zeus had already in mind the creation of the greatest hero the world was ever to know. He thusly had his favorite son Hermes tell Helios to stay home in the Colchis-- where he stabled his horses during the hours of dark--for three nights running, so that a penetration lasting that long would favor the river of semen he would ejaculate.

Having accomplished his task, the real Amphitryon returned to honor his bride but she refused as they had both just had fulfilling pleasure. Amphitryon, baffled, consulted the seer Teiresias who told him what had taken place. Amphitryon, afraid of offending Zeus, would never come near Alcmene again.

Nine months after Zeus' three-night-long visit, Heracles saw the light of day and Zeus, seeing that he would never again make a more superior being, left mortal women untouched from that time onwards, to Hera's great relief. Alcmene decided to expose the boy through fear of Zeus, and left him outside the walls of Thebes. It was there that Athena, who had been born from the head of her cherished father Zeus, led Hera, under Zeus' orders. Pointing out the beautiful child to Hera, and knowing that Hera was at that moment rich in breast milk, Athena suggested that she save the boy by giving him a suck. Heracles being Heracles, he chomped down so violently on Hera's breast that she hollered out in pain, backing off and releasing a surge of milk so great that it formed our Milky Way. She huffed off but the deed was done, thanks to her milk and Zeus' semen the boy was

Immortal. Athena told Alcmene she had nothing to fear from Zeus and that she was to feed the boy from that moment on, which she did.

Heracles suckling at Hera's breast.

Heracles' exploits began early. At age eight months Hera, furious at having been tricked, sent serpents to destroy him. It was the boy who bit off the heads of the snakes. Amphitryon adopted the lad and taught him the art of war and self-defense. Heracles cut a club from an olive tree and went abroad naked as the day until he killed the lion and won the splendid shepherd lad Molorchos. Heracles never looked for trouble but the times were difficult and trouble always seemed to search him out, especially as he sowed to the four winds, as the Greeks say of those who favor carnal pleasures. He took girls and wives who crossed his path, not a difficult task as the lion pelt he wore did little to cover the considerable free-swinging appendage at the confluent of his thighs, an enticement to both sexes. He gave Megaea eight sons. He had the King of Euboea torn in half by being roped between two horses when he came between Heracles and one of his loves. Hera never gave up trying to destroy him, and once she made him go mad, the time it took for him to kill six of his sons by still another maiden. As the Roman Caesar would later succumb to the charms and experience of King Nicomedes, so too did Heracles, still a boy, succumb to the King of Argos, Eurystheus, who made him become aware of every erogenous zone of his body. In gratitude, Heracles put himself under the king's orders, the basis of the Twelve Labors. Zeus' two preferred sons, Hermes and Apollo, gave Heracles a sword and a bow and arrows.

The *Argo,* constructed by Argus, was an open boat, a galley, of fifty rowers and a huge mainsail. As Zeus' wife Hera and Athena were very close, they worked in tandem with Argus on the ship's construction. Athena provided the prow, an enormous timber taken from the site of her sacred

Oracle, Dodona, and itself had powers of prophesy. Thanks to Athena's design beams were bolted in place, making the vessel as strong as steel and impossible to sink, and the boat's lines were so exquisite that she cut through the water with barely a stir, going sweetly forward when under oar by the crew of Hellas' best boys, or when under wind.

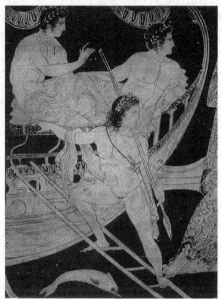

Men of the *Argo*

We'll learn about the crew of the *Argo* as we go along. For the moment we've introduced Jason, the shipbuilder Argus and Heracles, about whom we'll learn still more later. We'll learn, for example, that Jason's lover Hylas, in the first bloom of youth, was aboard. The Greeks often referred to these lover-belovèd twosomes by saying that the boy was the squire of the man, or that he was the man's arrow carrier and the keeper of his bow. This was Hylas' function until Heracles boarded. The boy then exchanged Jason, barely a man, for Heracles who well knew how to scratch a lad where it itched the most.

As Theognis tells us:

Boys and horses have the same brain.
A horse doesn't cry when the rider bites the dust.
He goes off with another who will sate him with seed.
The same with a boy eating from the hand of a new friend.

Ovid assures us that Hylas was, in reality, Heracles' son. There are some men who, for reasons unknown to mere mortals, are beyond the circle of life, as are infants and the very old. Common rules and morality have no hold on them. Such was the case of the poet Byron who impregnated his sister and got her with child, as the ancients put it, and was caught forcing an entrance into a girl of eleven, prevented in time by her mother, Byron's mistress, Lady Oxford. (2) Such was Heracles too.

Jason and his men, ready to fetch the Golden Fleece, said their goodbyes. Jason's mother Alcimede, who had lost Jason once when forced to fake his death and send him to Cheiron the Centaur was aghast at the thought of losing him again. She decried her plight, sobbing that her last wish had been for her boy's cherished hands to lay her body to eternal rest at the time of her death. Jason gently chided her for so burdening his soul before the departure. From his bed his aged father Aeson stifled his moans and offered his blessing. Jason tore himself away and joined his companions outside, each biting at the bit like yearlings eager to be off. The hearts of these young men were brimming with joy as they were off to explore the vast world beyond Iolcus, to know hope and promise and adventures, new lands and new peoples. They were in high spirits too because they knew they had the blessings of Hera and Athena. Who could have foreseen that Phrixus' sacrificing of a ram would lead to this, although small events are always the cause of great happenings.

Argo

As they left the town limits they felt enlivened by the thought that the old had been left behind by the young. All of Iolcus--inhabitants, friends, lovers and children--traipsed behind the warriors as they made their way to the beach of Pagasea, singing and waving fronds. The *Argo* bobbed in the harbor, fully decked out with banners, flags and pennants, its sides covered with the shields of all the participating countries. Perfume burners and fires in bronze vessels consumed incense in such quantity that the air was misty. Lovers and friends kissed goodbye and the boys went off to their fates.

Some of the men had shown especially great courage in coming. Idmon, for example, was the son of Apollo who had been taught to read the future through the observation of birds and the study of burned offerings. From this he knew he would perish should he enter the *Argo*. Mopsus had been taught to prophesy and knew that both he and his inseparable friend Canthus would find death in far-off Libya, proof that there was no escape from the Grim Reaper, even at the very end of the earth. These men knew their fates and went willingly.

The first stopover of the *Argo* was the island of Lemnos. Now, the Lemnians were stranger than fiction. When the men could no longer put up with their wives whom they accused of stinking to the extent of making them untouchable, they simply ejected them from the household and replaced them with Thracian women. The consequence was terrible. In the dead of night the Lemnian harridans massacred them all in their sleep. At first they were drunk with their new powers and freedom from male tyranny. They donned the men's external symbols of their might, their body armor, shields, daggers and swords. They met passing ships in this fashion, flashing their swords and spears. Taken for men thanks to their helmeted heads, no ship dared land.

When one of the oldest women among them finally realized that without men there would be no renewal of the population, they decided to hail the next passing boat, shucking their armor in favor of their girlish forms. The boat happened to be the *Argo* and the women, hungry for men after a year of abstinence, welcomed the lads as later the Tahitians would honor Captain Cook and his crew, giving themselves on the sand even as they debarked. As Lemnos was known for its wine--and would be the source of wine for the Greek forces heading for the greatest battle in the history of the world, that which would take place at Troy--the bacchanalias that followed would surpass all those still to come: Orgies under Dionysus, competitions sponsored by Messaline, the lavish debauch of the participants of the Borgia Banquet of the Chestnuts, and revels offered by Cheiron the Centaur. There were 48 boys and several hundred starved females. Only lusty Heracles stayed away on the *Argo* with Hylus, which does not mean he was less lusty and less preoccupied than his shipmates.

They all gained the hearth of their oars a week later, their heads heavy with drink, their balls pleasantly empty and their brains wondrously clear. Jason had been honored by the queen herself who would give birth to twins, one of whom, Eurneus, would become king and would cleanse the island of bloodguilt by rituals and new fire brought from the island of Delos, sacred to Apollo.

Scenes from Lemnos.

From Lemnos they sailed through the Hellespont at night so as to avoid being seen by mighty Troy that controlled the passage through its waters. They went to Arcton where they were welcomed by King Cyzicus, the son of Aeneas, who especially welcomed Heracles as he knew that both Heracles and his father had been lovers when at the court of Cheiron the Centaur, a hopelessly sentimental matchmaker. As Cyzicus had just married, the Argonauts were in time for the enormous banquet, a dozen tables adorned with every kind of food, especially roasted pig, and the best wines. Under the veil of night they retired to the beach to swim naked in the light of the moon and sport as youths are like to do when wine eases all inhibitions. They set off a week later, thanking Cyzicus and his bride for their reception. Alas, a storm came up and it was in the dead of pitch-black night that they were blown to a shore where villagers sounded the alarm, certain the *Argo* was a ship of pirates come to despoil them. Unknown to one and all, the landfall was again Arcton. Cyzicus and his men came out to do battle, guided only by the light of newly appearing stars on the glistening Argonaut armor. Both sides fought courageously but Cyzicus was run through by Jason himself. The mistake was discovered by the first rays of Eos, Helios' sister the Dawn. Cyzicus was given proper burial during which his new bride, mad with grief, hanged herself. Games were ordered in honor of Cyzicus, during which Idmon noticed the appearance of a bird, a halcyon. As he knew the language of birds he was able to direct the Argonauts in the propitious libations they offered to the gods, making sure that none was forgotten. Two oxen were chosen, one felled by Heracles, victim to his club, the other bludgeoned by an axe wielded by Ancaeus, whose great honor it was to be seated next to Heracles on the *Argo*. The throats were slit and the beasts' precious blood soaked into the sand of the beach. The flesh was carved up, the thighs were covered with a layer of fat and burned in honor of the Immortal gods.

As Helios descended and dusky shadows from the rocks fell across the beach, the lads spread out on beds of leaves. Warned by fires and the abundance of food and wine, they comforted each other with stories of courageous deeds, as boys are like to do in each other's company. Jason fell mysteriously silent, as the precariousness of his youth--Pelias who had wanted him dead, and the mother and father who had given him up to the Centaur Cheiron--and this challenge that would test his ability to guide these honorable and dangerous men, gave him an inner life of grave uncertainty. Idas tried to bring him out of his shell by promising to be at his side, offering protection that even the gods could not provide. This brought on a rough retort by Idmon who accused Idas of blasphemy. Peleus intervened, and with soothing words brought peace and rejuvenating sleep to these boys far from home yet content to be among friends.

The story of Peleus is largely intertwined with that of Cheiron the Centaur. Cheiron, as stated, was King of the Centaurs but unlike them his front quarters were human, a human bust and human legs. He was Zeus' half-brother whose father Cronus had taken the form of a horse to cover the maiden Philyra, Cheiron's mother. Centaurs were similar to satyrs in having long ears that rose above the head, as well as a predilection for drink and bacchanalias during which they straddled both sexes. Cheiron himself was of a gentle nature and his concept of boy-love was that of the Greeks, based on the education of their beloveds. It was thusly that he took a personal hand in the instruction of Jason, Achilles, Asclepius, Heracles, Theseus, Aias, Telamon and Aeneas. It was Cheiron who brought Telamon and Heracles together, and blessed their love. His diet was milk, but should he become exposed to drink his natural wild side came through and all except those who craved his brutality fled from his presence. It was Cheiron who introduced Peleus to Thetis.

Cheiron teaching his boys, step by step,
what they needed to know to become men.

Peleus was Telamon's brother. They had had another brother too, Phocus, a lad privileged by their father because he was an excellent athlete who turned the heads of his companions thanks to his exploits and beauty. Mad with jealousy, Peleus and Telamon waylaid the boy and smashed in his head with an axe. As related above, it was Heracles who offered Telamon his wife Hesione after killing Laomedon, King of Troy, replacing him with the boy Priam.

Peleus fled to the court of Phthia where he was offered the king's daughter Polymela in marriage and where he inadvertently speared the king's son while out boar hunting. He fled again to Ioclus with Polymela where our story had begun. Here Peleus was received by Acastus, son of Pelias, whose wife tried to lure him into her bed. When this didn't succeed she told Polymela that Peleus had tried to rape her. Believing the story, Polymela hanged herself. As Acastus had no proof of his guilt, he challenged Peleus to a hunt, the result of which would decide his guilt or innocence in the attempted rape of his wife. Peleus slaughtered a great number of beasts but Acastus nonetheless declared that it was he who had killed the most, and prepared to murder Peleus. Luckily Peleus had cut out the tongues of the animals he had shot and, opening his hunting bag, let them spill out at Acastus' feet. "Let these tongues reveal the identity of the winner," Peleus declared. That night Acastus set a horde of centaurs against Peleus who bound him during his sleep and carried him away to be sacrificed. Luckily Cheiron was warned and saved Peleus in the nick of time.

The *Argo* rowed on in the direction of Colchis. The days were long, hot and of stifling boredom. Heracles had an idea that would both relieve the dullness and get them to their destination faster. He initiated a contest between the Argonauts, the winner of which would be he who could row the longest. The enthusiasm was immediate, even if it meant doing what they had all been doing all along, but as we know, boys will pick up on any and every challenge. They rowed until there were finally only four contenders left, Heracles, of course, Jason too, as was apt since he was the leader, and Castor and Polydeuces, twins, known as the Dioscuri.

Now, we all know about the Trojan War, the cause of which was Helen's boredom until Paris came to her in a dream, his chiton delightfully distended by the arch of his manhood as he bent over Helen's luscious naked breasts. A dream that would soon, thanks to the diabolical tandem of Athena and Hera, become reality. Well, Helen had a sister and two twin brothers. The father of all four was Tyndareus who impregnated his wife Leda, his sperm fertilizing half of two of Leda's eggs. She immediately went to a nearby stream to cleanse herself, where she saw the most wonderful swan her eyes had beheld. Its wide beak caressed her inner thighs, prolonging the pleasure of her sport with Tyndareus, and she literally swooned when the swan forced a passage with his black head and the full length of its thick white neck. Thusly did Zeus fertilize the unspoiled half of her two eggs, which divided into four parts, two of which were Tyndareus's and would by-and-by produce Clytaemnestra and Castor, the other two eggs inseminated by the god producing Helen and Polydeuces, both immortal. The two girls were twins but life's abuse of Clytaemnestra, in the form of her callous husband Agamemnon, left here indifferent to her physical envelope, whereas Helen worshipped her own body, pampering and bronzing it--unheard of for women, normally lily white--into the form that would eventually launch a thousand ships.

As for Castor and Polydeuces, they were inseparable rival brothers who turned their bronzed bodies into mechanical perfection. Tyndareus, by the way, was King of Sparta, and his sons were Sparta's greatest pride. Castor specialized in soldiering and horse taming and riding, Polydeuces was a great fighter. Both were athletes who won many an Olympic prize. These boys had two cousins who were also aboard the *Argo*, Idas, already mentioned, and Lynceus. Later on they would have a falling out over cattle they had together rustled. Idas would run Castor through with his spear and in revenge the immortal Polydeuces would spear both Idas and Lynceus. Castor went to Hades and Zeus called Polydeuces to Mount Olympus to join him. Polydeuces refused, stating he would go nowhere without his brother. Finally, it was agreed that both brothers would go to Heaven and Hell on alternating days. In recognition of their brotherly love Zeus had their stars placed in orbit, and Poseidon named them Saviors of shipwrecked sailors and Bestowers of favorable winds.

But for the moment they're racing in order to win the competition for best rower. Eventually Castor gave out and Polydeuces threw down his oar in disgust at his brother's weakness. Jason was decided on dying at the oar before giving up and he would have done so had he not fainted dead away. At that exact same moment Heracles' oar broke and he let out a very vile oath that surprised no one as these young men, largely thanks to the extremely randy women on Lemnos, had by now heard and seen it all. They beached the *Argo* at the mouth of the river Chius and collapsed on the sandy banks in pure exhaustion.

Here occurred the saddest event of the expedition, one that would mark Heracles for life. To refresh his lover, Hylas decided to go off in search of fresh cool water. When he didn't return Heracles, mad with fear that he had been waylaid by robbers, went off looking for him. It turned out that Hylas had wandered to a spring guarded by nymphs, one of whom, Mysia, fell in love with the boy. As he reached over to fill his amphora she reached up for a kiss. Hylas lost his balance and Mysia, thinking he dove into the pool to offer her more than a kiss, pulled him down to her watery abode, unaware that by doing so she would kill him.

The story of Hylas is similar to that of Bormus, an extraordinarily beautiful boy who, during harvest time, went for water for himself and his harvester buddies. Then too, as he bent over a pool of cool spring water, nymphs pulled him into its depths to satisfy their lust. Bormus was a Bithynian, a land famous for its handsome lads, the most famous of which was Antinous.

Now, Calais and Zetes were Argonauts and twins too, like the Dioscuri, whose father was Boreas, the serpent-tailed North Wind who had destroyed the Persian King Xerxes' fleet, earning him a temple and worshippers. But he was also a randy bastard who loved mares and often changed himself into a black horse that blew over dozens at a time, impregnating them all. It was Calais and Zetes who convinced Jason that they mustn't wait for the return of Heracles and Polyphemus, who had gone off to help Heracles find Hylas, but instead take the favorable wind that now offered itself. Jason agreed and they set sail anew for the land of Colchis and the Golden Fleece. But these three were alone in their wish to abandon Heracles. Telamon, Heracles' former lover, would have come to blows with Jason had not Calais and Zetes held him back, aided by their powerful wings. The crew knew, too, that should the two wish to invoke the aid of their father Boreas, the North Wind, the ship would go nowhere. As the expedition chief, Jason won the day, but more than one of the crew mumbled that Jason was getting even for losing the rowing contest against Heracles, while others hinted that he was just plain jealous of Heracles' invincibility.

But Heracles was not invincible and the time has come to say farewell to him. Yet before, just a word about the loyal Polyphemus who had remained to help his friend find his belovèd boy. In gratitude Zeus would later give him rule over a town to be called Mysia, after the nymph who so loved Hylas. Calais and Zetes did not fare so well. Returning from the funeral of Pelias they were waylaid by Heracles who, in vengeance for their refusal to have the *Argo* wait for him until he found Hylas, bludgeoned both to death with his club. As far as Heracles himself, his end was markedly unworthy of a hero of the Twelve Labors and an Argonaut. One day he was wandering around the countryside with his wife when he came upon a rampant river. A seemingly gentle centaur named Nessus offered to carry Heracles' wife, Deianeira, across it. Heracles thanked him and began to swim to the other side, confident that Nessus was following with Deianeira on his back. When Heracles reached the opposite bank, however, he was aghast to see his wife still on the further shore, in the clutches of the centaur who had straddled her.

Heracles shot an arrow across the river that pierced Nessus in the neck, causing him to withdraw at the moment of his pleasure, and ejaculate over Deianeira's thighs. Before dying, the centaur, who knew of Heracles' fondness for both sexes, told Deianeira that if she dipped Heracles' shirt in a mixture made from the centaur's blood and seed, she would never have to worry about her husband being unfaithful again. Deianeira took the advice, putting the liquids in a jar and hiding it.

Years later, Deianeira, now old, learned that Heracles was making a sacrifice at Zeus' temple in the company of still another youth. Eaten by jealousy, she decided to use the centaur's mixture as a love-potion to win him back. Heracles sent to Deianeira for a clean shirt to wear to the sacrifice. Deianeira took a new one from the chest and, with the aid of a piece of cloth, covered the shirt with the mixture. She then tossed the piece of cloth outside, and sent the shirt to her husband.

Moments later her attention was drawn to the sunlit courtyard by something blazing like reflecting bronze. There she saw the piece of cloth enveloped in fire. Realizing that the centaur had tricked her, she sent to stop the shirt from being delivered to Heracles.

She was too late. Heracles was before Zeus' altar in his new shirt when the heat from the burning sacrifice caused it to erupt into flames. Seized by overpowering pain, he tried to pull away the garment. Only his own flesh, bleeding and corroding, came loose. Mad with suffering, he tore at himself until the bones of his bloody arms and pearl-white ribs were laid bare. To escape the agony, he begged his friends to place his body on a pyre so he could end his days before being turned into a mindless half-wit by the eroding fluid.

The pyre was built and Heracles placed on top, but no one dared to light it for fear lest he change his mind and strike him dead. By chance a shepherd passing by consented to put a torch to the funeral pyre. This was Philoctetes, and in thanks Heracles gave him his bow and arrows. The swirling flames brought an end to the great hero and to his wife, Deianeira, who threw herself into the blaze out of grief.

Philoctetes, by the way, was one of Heracles' many ancient lovers, and his personal destiny is a must in the annals of Trojan history:

It had been predicted that Philoctetes and his bow and arrows were necessary if the Greeks wished to topple mighty Tory. Because the bow and arrows had belonged to Heracles, and Hera hated him because he was the greatest of her husband Zeus' bastards, she did whatever she could to destroy Philoctetes. Now, Philoctetes, on his way to Troy, was bitten by Hera who had taken the form of a serpent--an effortless disguise for one as two-tongued as she. This took place on the island of Lemnos where Philoctetes offered a sacrifice in memory of Heracles. Hera, rabid with anger that anybody should so honor one of Zeus' lovechildren, turned herself into a viper and bit him. Philoctetes did not succumb to his wound, however, but it festered so badly that the Greeks, repelled by the stink, were forced to leave him behind on Lemnos. Here is the scene that follows, as related by the poet:

A large inclining plank was held two feet above the sand by a sturdy stake. A vine led from the bottom of the stake to a clump of bushes several yards away, where it disappeared into the foliage. Scattered on the sand beneath the plank were sunflower seeds that a small black and yellow bird was ravenously pecking up. Suddenly there was a slight flurry from the bushes, the vine went taut, the stake was pulled out from under the plank, and the plank fell mutely to the sand. So encased was the little bird that not even the cracking of its bones was heard by the torrid sun or the swaying eucalyptus around the shimmering lagoon.

Out from under the bushes came a figure dressed in rags. He pulled himself forward, like a land crab, on heavily-muscled forearms, his left leg dragging uselessly behind. Over the sand he skittered to the fallen trap from whence he extracted the soggy little bird. He made a deep, hungry groan in his throat, but decided to put away the tidbit in his quiver until later in the afternoon, when it would help him get through the night should he have trapped nothing else.

He skittered back to the beach that bordered the clear lagoon in search of tiny fish, small sea shrimps and the plethora of shelled animals that were often caught in the shallow pools of warm water at low tide. He hesitated motionless before each basin while his eyes fleetingly sought out any movement that indicated life. It was then that his attention was caught by something on the horizon. He frowned into the distance, forcing his eyes to focus leagues beyond the normal sight of men. He clucked his tongue in wild satisfaction and began to whisper to himself rapidly.

"They're coming! Hallelujah! They're coming, they're coming! Just like Heracles promised: "The ships'll be back, old Philoctetes," he said. "They'll need those arrows and that bow of yours. Just keep yourself calm, sane and fed." That's what old Heracles said and he was right. Here they come, and that's lying old Odysseus at the helm. "Watch out for that double-dealing runt," Heracles warned, "Don't let him get within a serpent's tail of your bow and arrows." Oh, you can bet I won't, immortal son of Zeus! Where my darts go, I go. Who's that beside Odysseus? Ah, Diomedes. Now, there's a brave bugger. But what's he doing in such disreputable company? There's something strange, strange, strange a foot. We'll see if they outfox old Philoctetes. Machaon is there too, on the prow. He's been sent to cure my leg. I hope he's come up with some miracle drug over the past ... how many years? Mercy, I've no idea ... a hundred, I suppose. I'd better bathe before they get here. I can't let them see me looking like this."

Without further ado, Philoctetes threw himself into the lagoon--rags and all, splashed about a bit, and then pulled himself out of its pleasant, caressing waters. Rivulets ran down his sticky hair and the wet shreds he vainly tried to ring dry. He pulled himself back up the beach and into the trees where his branch and leaf hut squatted. He collected his bow and filled his quiver with arrows. He was now in tiptop shape to honor the Greek delegation.

The men weren't long in coming. They were walking along the shore when Philoctetes suddenly dropped from his hiding place to greet them.

"We meet again," Philoctetes called, too loudly. He nearly turned a somersault, so surprised was he at hearing his own voice.

"Philoctetes!" cried Odysseus. "We'd given you up for lost. I told Machaon here that we'd scour all Ocean until we found our friend."

"I haven't left Lemnos. Why didn't you begin your scouring here?"

"We did," interceded Diomedes. "We couldn't come before because it's only now that Machaon received a shipment of wonder medicines from Cheiron the Centaur."

"Well, it's not too early," said Philoctetes as he glanced at his poor leg trailing behind him. The putrid stink that rose from the foot wound turned their stomachs.

"You're looking well," commented Odysseus to the old, salt-white, mangy carcass of bones that filled Philochetes' rags.

"You haven't changed much yourself," retorted Philoctetes.

"Let me take those arrows," said Odysseus, advancing towards him. "You don't need them for hunting now that your friends are here. Besides, you may cut yourself on their sharp points, and begin your run of bad luck all over again."

"Stand back!" cried out Philoctetes, stringing one.

"Have you gone mad!" yelled Odysseus, stopped dead in his tracks. "This isn't the good Philoctetes we left on Lemnos nine years ago!"

"But it's the one you find. Be prepared for changes in those you neglect or forget."

"We came to heal you, Philoctetes," said Diomedes. "We obviously can't if you're going to keep an arrow trained on us all the time."

"I'll let you and Machaon care for me, but not him," said the old man, pointing out Odysseus. "You come and prop me up against that tree there, Diomedes. And you fix my foot, Machaon. As for *him*, he's to stay in the middle of the beach where I can keep an eye trained on his shifty face."

The two men did as Philoctetes ordered, fighting off the irresistible urge to vomit. Philoctetes' foot was an unbelievable sight after nine years of neglect. It reminded Machaon of a case of advanced leprosy; he couldn't figure out why it hadn't dropped off ages before. Odysseus stayed prudently back, and while Machaon dressed Philoctetes' foot, Diomedes joined him. Philoctetes began to yelp with pain.

"Go to Machaon and assist him in nursing the old fart," said Odysseus. "Pretend to be helpful, but when Machaon isn't looking, squeeze the wound for all you're worth. The moment Philoctetes faints, pluck away his bow and arrows and bring them to me."

"Why can't we take the old duffer with us to Troy? The prophecy will be fulfilled and we won't have to hurt him."

"If we take back Philoctetes, we'll be stranded here for weeks while we wait for his wound to heal."

"But Agamemnon said..."

"Do as *I* say!"

Diomedes returned to the patient but refused to add to Philoctetes' misery. Nevertheless, Philoctetes began to succumb to the pain and very slowly his hold on his armed bow became less and less firm. His eyes flickered open and shut, the moments when they were closed becoming longer and longer until he passed out. Odysseus had been inching forward bit by bit and now came at his former companion like an eagle swooping down on an abandoned nest of baby field shrews. He would have succeeded, too, in wrenching the bow and arrows from Philoctetes' feeble grip had not the great demigod Heracles appeared at that very moment.

"I know you!" he roared at Odysseus. The poor Ithacan quaked before the muscled giant who wore the skull of a lion on his head and its skin around his body, tied closed at his neck and around his waist by the animal's paws. "And I know what you're after! So buzz off if you don't want your face pushed out through your asshole." Then turning to Machaon he asked: "What's that on his foot?"

"A plaster of herbs, wild plants and drugs that will heal the wound."

"Philoctetes is to be cured in order for him to accompany you to Troy," ordered Heracles. "You all remember how I first went to that honorless city. I rescued Priam's aunt, Hesione, from the sea monster's deadly grip. She was supposed to have become my bride but Laomedon refused to hand her over. In retaliation I burned Troy, beheaded Laomedon, made off with Hesione and gave her to my friend Telamon. I then appointed Priam to succeed his father. At that time he wasn't more than a sparrow-chested tyke, but he didn't take long to make a mess of his reign. He built his city on the forbidden hill of Ate, one of his sons abducted a Spartan slut, and Priam himself raised hell over getting Hesione back--an old bag of eighty--thereby upsetting Telamon who's asked me to intervene in her memory, though what pleasure she gave him ... but that's another story.

"Now these are my words and they'd better be clear. Troy is to fall a second time to my arrows; I want it, I ordain it and by Zeus I shall have it! Philoctetes is to go back with you once he's fit, and it's he who's to do the shooting. If I hear of anyone so much as trying to harm the lice on his head, he'll answer to Heracles and," said the demigod, lowering his voice, *"I ... won't ... be ... gentle."*

With that, Heracles disappeared as mysteriously as he had come, leaving the men paralyzed, except for Philoctetes who regarded them all with a sly grin. (1)

The *Argo* sailed on to the isle of Bebrycos where its king was the psychopath Amycus, son of Poseidon. His fetish was to challenge young men to a boxing contest, and if they refused or if they lost they were thrown from a cliff to their deaths on the rocks below. Jason requested food and water but Amycus refused until Jason chose the best of the Argonauts to confront him. Polydeuces of the Dioscrui was picked, as he was a renowned boxer. Both men donned leathers gloves, but Amycus' were studded with spikes. Polydeuces kept his distance until he could judge the king's mannerisms and detect his weak points. This done, he weighed in with jabs and uppercuts, bloodying the tyrant's face until one blow to the nose drove the bone into his brain, followed by another that fractured the skull at the temple. Amycus was dead before he hit the earth, the earth eager to absorb the blood, more nourishing than water. In order to soothe Amycus' father Poseidon, the Astronauts stole the king's sheep and massacred twenty that they hauled before his altar in sacrifice. The rest of the herd and Amycus' wealth they divvied up among themselves in equal portions.

They went on to Salmydessus where the ruler was Phineus. Now, Phineus was an arrogant old man who had been given prophetic powers by Apollo and used them to disclose Zeus' every sacred move, especially those concerning the god's numerous infidelities. In revenge Zeus made him both blind and tormented by harpies, winged monsters whose purpose is to punish criminals. Whenever Phineus took a meal the harpies swooped down and shat upon every morsel. As Apollonius of Rhodes tells us in R.V. Rieu's wonderful translation of his *Argonautica*, Phineus's "shriveled flesh was caked with dirt, and his bones were held together only by the skin." But Phineus had lost none of his verve, addressing the Argonauts as the "flower of Hellenic chivalry." He filled their eager ears with promises that he would reveal the secrets of Colchis so as to facilitate their taking the Golden Fleece. In exchange, the Argonauts were to rid him of the harpies. A pact was concluded and the next time the harpies attacked, Calais and his brother Zetes, the winged sons of the North Wind Boreas, were waiting for them, armed with swords. They struck at the snapping fiends and forced them to flee to their home base, the Island of Return. Here they came upon Iris, their protector. She told Calais and Zetes that the harpies were Zeus' own hounds and were thusly sacrosanct. She did promise, though, that if the twins let up their chase, the harpies would leave Phineus in eternal peace. This was agreed to.

Having fulfilled the promise that Phineus would no longer be shat upon, Jason demanded his recompense, knowledge of what awaited them all at Colchis. Phineus warned them that the entrance to the Bosporus was guarded by mist-enshrouded rocks that crushed any and every ship that sailed between them. The rocks would come together, clash, and then separate, only to clash together once again. The way through, said Phineus, was to release a bird between the rocks. When these came into contact, hopefully only on the bird's tail feathers, the *Argo* was to surge forward, for the rocks were forced to open before being able to snap back again. This Jason and his crew did, amid the roar, spray and terrible surge caused by the rocks parting and closing. Only the stern of the *Argo* was slightly scraped, thanks to the superb steering of Tiphys, but the men knew a moment of pure fear that froze their hearts.

Now in the Black Sea, they knew, again thanks to Phineus, something of what awaited them: they would sail past the entrance to Hades itself, as well as along great rivers and promontories and bays, welcoming beaches and less welcoming Amazons, past tribes peaceful and tribes cannibalistic, and then on to Colchis itself. The men of the *Argo* had honored Phineus with a huge banquet and sacrifice, thanks to Amycus' sheep, in advance of which they had stripped Phineus naked and washed away the filth left by the harpies over years of abuse. The gods were not forgotten, Zeus, Hera and Athena, and, at Phineus' prodding, Aphrodite, who would play, said the prophet, a future role in their survival.

A Greek banquet. Can the reader imagine greater happiness?

The Amazons were female warriors, some of whom fought in the Trojan War while others, later, would fight alongside Mithriades against the Romans. Achilles killed one of their queens and Heracles killed twelve. They were said to have been of Scythian stock, and no greater warriors than the Scythians have ever fought under the heavens and upon the earth. They lived in the southern part of the Black Sea. One breast was cut away or cauterized so they could shoot arrows like a man. The other served to nurse their female babies, while male children were exposed to the elements, leaving their destiny to the gods. Others say they had no regard for decency, and broke the boys' limbs to ensure their deaths. Some believe they mated with neighboring tribes during two-months-long orgies the men appreciated because the women were so famished for male attention. Or they may have mated with slaves captured during combat, before their execution. Their hatred of men knew no limits, not surprising when one learns that Greek and Spartan women served as sperm vessels, as Apollo put it, just good for cooking and caring for children, as well as preparing the meals the men offered their boys, never hesitating to caress a lad's buttocks or fondle a chiton-covered prong in their presence.

Now on the Black Sea, the Argonauts, thrilled at having escaped death thanks to their shared courage, came ashore and sacrificed sheep in testimony of their shared oath to defend each other to the death, an oath that would inspire future generations, the basis of the Sacred Band of Thebes.

They sailed on to the town of Mariandyne where they were welcomed by King Lycus who had already received word of King Amycus' death. He organized a banquet during which he offered his son Dascyhlus as a guide for their future journey. The king also organized a hunt during which, alas, Idmon met his end under the circumstances he himself, as a seer, and foreseen. His thigh was opened by the tusk of a wild boar and he bled to death. Here too the steersman Tiphys came down with a fever and left the only world he had know, one of heartbreak and occasional joy. He was replaced by Ancaeus.

Sacrifices were performed and that night at a banquet Jason told King Lycus of their adventures, his return to his home at Ioclus and his reunion with his father and mother, of Pelias' promise to offer him the kingship in return for the Golden Fleece, the very purpose of their voyage, of Lemnos and the women's reception, a story that much pleased Lycus for he was still young and regaled in tales of sexual exploits, of their encounter with Amycus and the harpies and the Clashing Rocks, and their arrival at Mariandyne.

King Lycus congratulated them all and asked for news of Heracles. When filled in, he informed the crew that Heracles himself had passed through his lands when Lycus had the first down on his cheeks and had challenged his father to a friendly boxing match, during which he had knocked out all of his father's front teeth. But they had then struck up a friendship and Heracles had helped his father win over surrounding lands that were now Lycus' own.

They sailed on to Sinope, a city named after a maiden Zeus loved so much he promised he would grant her greatest wish. She asked to remain a virgin. Her wish granted, she spent her years in happy solitude. Here, too, the *Argo* took on three new crewmembers, Deilon, Phlogius and Autolycus. Autolycus was the son of clever Hermes and was a born thief that Hermes had taught to cover his tracks thanks to ingenious strategies. When he stole cattle, for example, he could make those with white become black, males become females, those with horns become hornless. Now, Autolycus came across someone as cunning as he, Sisyphus, his neighbor, who noticed that Autolycus' herds were increasing while he was losing his own. Sisyphus therefore had the initials SA carved into the hooves of his cattle, meaning Stolen by Autolycus. He followed the prints in the dust which led to Autolycus' stables where, while the friends engaged in heated discussion outside, Sisyphus entered Autolycus' home and seduced his daughter, who would give birth to Odysseus, the wiliest of all the men destined to do battle before the gates of mighty Troy. Autolycus' daughter, by the way, was the wife of Laertes, who was already a crewmember of the *Argo*. Sisyphus, after taking his pleasure with Autolycus' daughter, donned his chiton and returned home. Autolycus, on the other hand, continued his misdeeds, even stealing cattle that he sold to Heracles. When the owner of the cattle accused Heracles of the robbery, Heracles took him to the top of the tower of his castle and asked him if he could see any cows from his herd. As Autolycus had changed their appearance, the owner could only shake his head. Angry for having been taken for a common thief, Heracles pushed the poor man to his death. If the reader hasn't guessed so already, I can assure you that Heracles was a psychopath, killing not only his children when moved to do so, but any man, woman or animal that crossed his path.

Later Autolycus would be present when his daughter gave birth to Odysseus and was asked to name the boy. Autolycus declared that as he had angered a great many people during his life, he would call the boy the Angry One, Odysseus in Greek.

A word concerning Sisyphus. In school I had been taught to honor this personage because of his unfailing willpower that encouraged him to keep pushing a rock up a hill even when he knew it would fall back as soon as he approached the top. Well, Sisyphus had a brother he hated so much that he consulted the Oracle of Delphi to find a way to rid himself of his presence. The Oracle told Sisyphus that if he impregnated his brother's daughter, her children by Sisyphus would kill his brother. This Sisyphus did. The woman bore him two sons, but when she learned of their destiny--that they would become murderers of their father--she killed them instead.

One of Sisyphus' boys by his legitimate wife, a lad named Glaucus, was so crazy about horse racing that he taught his horses to eat flesh, a purveyor of immense energy. But when he nonetheless lost a race, the animals--who had been held back in order for Glaucus to win a wager--turned on him and ate him alive. Another son, Sinon, so smooth he could entice the birds from the trees, was at Troy where he convinced the Trojans to allow the entry of the Wooden Horse into the city.

Sisyphus' triumphs were against the gods themselves, and no one was more guileful. When Asopus, son of Poseidon, sought to learn who had kidnapped his daughter, Sisyphus volunteered the information on condition that Asopus provide a never-ending source of water for the city Sisyphus ruled as king, Corinth. Asopus agreed and Sisyphus named Zeus himself as the kidnapper. Zeus was furious when found out. In revenge, he sent Death himself to do Sisyphus in. But ever-clever Sisyphus somehow persuaded Death to try on a pair of handcuffs, from which Sisyphus refused to free him. With Death in captivity no one could die, no matter how ghastly their wounds. Those beheaded, those executed by being pulled apart by horses, those looking forward to a peaceful afterlife on the Iles of the Blessed, all were obliged to await the freeing of Death so their destinies could find completion and their suffering come to an end. Finally Ares god of War was forced to intervene because the undead were piling up on the battlefields. He found and released Death and sent Sisyphus straight to Hell where his eternal punishment, as related, was to push, forever, a rock uphill.

The Argonauts continued on to the Isle of Ares where they found four shipwrecked men, all sons of Phrixus whose mother was the daughter of King Aeetes of Colchis, he who was at present guarding the Golden Fleece. These boys were Cytisorus, Argeus, Phrontis and Melanion. The boys had shipwrecked during a terrible storm of winds and high seas. Their vessel had sunk and the lads had made it to shore thanks to a huge beam they had all grasped on to. They had just come from Colchis, and when Jason informed them of the *Argo*'s mission, the four were not nearly as optimistic as Jason concerning the facility with which Jason thought King Aeetes would hand the Golden Fleece over. Aeetes was the son of Helios, they warned Jason, and had innumerable followers. Besides, the Fleece was guarded by a sleepless, deathless dragon, the offspring of Mother Earth and Tartarus who had produced the greatest monster ever, Typhon, he who was made of swirling serpents from the waist down. Zeus had tried to counter Typhon's power, first by unsuccessfully using the scythe that his father Cronus had used to castrate his own father Uranus, then by hurtling thunderbolts that wounded it, and from whose blood sprang the dragon that kept watch over the Golden Fleece. Later Zeus succeeded in harnessing Typhon's power by covering him with Mount Aetna, from which flows lava and fire to this very day. Jason replied, brightly, that they were strong enough to bend Aeetes to their will.

They sailed past the lofty peaks of the Caucasus where Prometheus was chained.

From the Caucasus they rowed past the island of Philyra where Cronus, Zeus' father, had lain, disguised as a horse, with Philyra, who gave birth to Cheiron the Centaur. When she saw the monster issued from her womb, she had herself metamorphosed into a tree.

Near the entrance to Hades Sthenelus, son of Actor, one of Heracles' uncountable loves, came forth in the form of a ghost, having begged Persephone, wife of Hades, to allow him to glimpse the men of the *Argo*. The crew was deeply impressed by the sight of the phantom and although he soon disappeared, they agreed to shore the boat and offer the specter a sacrifice of Amycus' sheep. Here Orpheus made an offering of his own, his dear lyre, after which the place would be eternally known as Lyra. The moment is perhaps propitious to tell the story of this man, Orpheus, known as the very first proselytizer of boy-love:

Orpheus could charm the spots off a leopard. Thanks to his lyre and beautiful voice streams ceased to trickle, rocks cried and trees danced, wrote Simonides of Ceos. Birds interrupted their songs, claimed Pindar. The Oracle of Delphi told Jason to include Orpheus among the Argonauts, which he was thankful for doing as no ship had ever been able to sail pass the Sirens, whose songs enticed sailors to shipwreck against their rocky home. But Orpheus played his lyre so wonderfully that the sounds from the Sirens never reached the men's ears, so enhanced were they by Orpheus' music.

On his wedding day Orpheus' wife Eurydice was bitten by a snake and died. At her funeral Orpheus' mournful songs caused even the gods to weep. They suggested that he go to the slime-walled caverns of the Underworld and beg Hades for her return. So he went to the river Styx where he charmed Hades' watchdog, the three-headed Cerberus, to let him through to Chiron, the ferryman who paddled the newly deceased across the vile waters from which none returned. Frightened bats fought for hiding places as Orpheus made his way through the most inaccessible, putrid side-shafts, the hotbed of the death maggots, to Hades' throne. There, his playing and singing softened the rock-hard heart of the foulest of the gods, he who placed his foot on the chests of brave warriors and tore out their souls from their still-warm bodies. Hades permitted him to return to the Upperworld with his sweetheart, as long as he never looked back to make certain she was indeed following. At the entrance, though, he did turn his head, in time to see her vanish into the noisome mists.

Decided to never again undergo such pain, he transferred his love to boys--boys not men--boys whose early flowering and springtime, says Ovid, is so brief. He spent three years as Apollo's priest at Delphi where he readied himself to propagate the cult of the god of Light. Apollo told him about Hyacinth and the joy of running, swimming and laughing with carefree lads, exercising, imparting knowledge and rolling in the deep grass with sturdy, corn-fed bucks as frisky and proud as stallions. As Orpheus was Apollo's best acolyte, Apollo sent him to the most difficult land in Greece, that of the Thracians, a barbarous people who went stark naked because they knew of the contamination that filthy clothing brought to wounds received in warfare. He revealed to them that the love of boys kept one eternally young, thanks to their innocence, and it is said that he showed the way by having many, many belovèds. He made the Thracians exchange cannibalism for fruit, and human sacrifice for rites similar to that of the Spartans, rites far less savage than human flesh eating but far more erotic too. He helped them found towns and organize themselves. The Thracians made huge strides, even if they still remained more heathen than other Greeks. The proof is that even in more recent times, during the life of Alcibiades, Athens had engaged Thracians as mercenaries but were forced to let them return home without pay because the city had gone bankrupt. The Thracians returned through Boeotia, a land to the north of Athens. Along the way they massacred every living thing, Thucydides tells us, men, women and children, boys in their schools and beasts of burden. ''Nothing was so unexpected and loathsome,'' ends Thucydides, whose disgust is easily felt and seconded.

It was then that Orpheus undertook the voyage as an Argonaut, during which he met the young and handsome Calais, ''a boy he loved,'' according to the poet Phanocles. But their idyll was not to last. This time it wasn't the youth who died but Orpheus himself. He returned to Thrace with Calais and found that the Thracians had backslid. Most had returned to the rites of the Maenads, Dionysian maidens who enticed the Thracians into wild orgies when under the influence of their god's wine. The Maenads immediately attempted to entice Orpheus and Calais with naked breasts and spread thighs, but met only disgust from the man and the boy. In revenge they fell on Orpheus with tooth and nail, tearing him to pieces. Fleet footed Calais escaped and joined his twin brother Zetes, both later killed by Heracles who accused them both of hindering him when he went off in search of *his* belovèd, Hylas. The Muses gathered up the remains of Orpheus and buried them at the foot of Mount Olympus where nightingales eternally sing over his grave. His lyre was placed in the heavens as a constellation and his soul was, later, reunited with that of Calais in the Elysian Fields.

After having sacrificed to the ghost of Sthenelus, outside the entrance to Hades, they sailed past the land of the Amazons. From the *Argo* they saw the black smoke-filled skies over the land of the Chalybes, men who dug iron and produced metal day after day, which they sold to provide themselves with food. The *Argo* rounded the promontory of the Tibereni where men went into labor when their wives gave birth, moaning and screaming, as their wives lovingly fulfilled their every wish. They saw the mountains of the Mossynoeci who did everything proper in the privacy of their own homes but reproduced like animals on the streets, in full view of their neighbors, but alas the crew could not draw near enough to enjoy the spectacle.

They went on to the river Phasis, on whose banks was the city of Colchis, their destination. They beached the *Argo* and offered thanks for their delivery, libations of sweet wine from gold cups to the gods and in memory of the lads who had not made it that far. They ate and prepared warm beds alongside he of his choice, and so sported and slept until Eos rose, blushing at the sight of young love entwined.

Areetes could not believe the presumption of the young men who requested, the next morning, that he return what was most valuable to his whole kingdom, the Golden Fleece. He told them he would burn the *Argo* and have the crews' tongues cut out as well as their hands and feet lopped off. Jason replied courteously, the worse possible action towards a man like Aeetes because it immediately deprived him of all his fire. "My lord Aeetes," began Jason. "We have come to you as suppliants, sent by a hard-hearted king. Pelias is his name and he wishes the return of the Fleece from the ram Phrixus had used to escape from Iolcus when wrongly accused of ravishing a woman he would not consent to love. Iolcus is now in the midst of a terrible drought that the Oracle of Delphi says will end only with the return of the Fleece. We are here to beg you to fulfill the prophecy by allowing us to return home with it. Believe me sir, your glory will be sung throughout all of Hellas."

Aeetes was soothed too by the appearance of the daughter he adored, Medea, who put an assuring hand on his shoulder. She looked, for the first time, at Jason. Aeetes lowered the tone and demanded that Jason, to prove he was worthy of the Fleece, yoke two monstrous fire-breathing bulls together and plow a nearby field. While Jason hesitated in giving a response, Medea studied him with dispassionate favor, for he was a comely lad of good height and build, a fresh face that pleased virgins. From his hideaway Eros, who wanted Jason to succeed in his endeavor, armed his bow and sent an arrow into Medea's breast that transpierced her right to the feathers. Invisible to all but the Immortals, Hera, Aphrodite and Athena, who also favored Jason, saw her heart stop. Love's sweat essence filled her body with fire, her cheeks reddened and her eyes engulfed the lithe boy before her, his own cheeks ruddy with virility, and a nascent beard as soft as silk and barely discernable for he was young and the down was new. His bronzed skin and muscular arms beckoned her mightily. Later those arms would encircle her in a gentle caress, so different from the manly give-and-take between Jason and his lovers, the Argonauts, whose white-hot scalding bodies fought as, in turn, each took his pleasure with the other.

From behind her father's shoulder Medea gave Jason a barely discernable nod, indicating that he acquiesce to Aeetes' demands.

Aided by the goddesses, Medea provided Jason with the oils that would keep him from being scortched by the fire-breathing bulls. She would apply the magic oil herself because should he do it and miss a spot, the bull would use it as an entry for his scalding flames. Thanks to his week with the Lemnians Jason allowed himself to be pampered, and thanks to what Medea had seen when boys were among themselves, she knew of the stroking that would bring Jason release. The oil and Medea's advice on how to mollify the beasts made the plowing of the fields an easy task, one he accomplished that afternoon. The next day, Jason--bathed and perfumed--strode again before King Aeetes. Neither the accomplishment of his task nor the beauty of the boy softened the king's heart, and he ordered Jason and his men out of his sight while he decided how to dispose of them. Medea, who had made shy acquaintance with the lad when she brought him the necessary items to win over the bulls, now came with the magic narcotics that she would sprinkle on the dragons eyes, as she was the only person the dragon allowed to approach him. In this way Jason was able to snatch the Golden Fleece, but not before being spotted by a priest responsible for the sanctuary, who sounded the alarm. Other priests arrived whom the crewmen put to death, but not before Meleager, Argus, Atalanta and Jason himself were wounded, and Iphitus killed.

The moment was a terrifying one for Medea. She knew her father would soon become aware of her role in the treachery as she had been unable to escape the watchful gaze of her many servants, maidens used to following a step behind her, and this from the time of her birth. She deeply, sincerely loved Jason, but she knew too the needs of men, of the countless mistresses taken by her father Aeetes, not only under the eyes of her mother, but her mother had warned her that this too would be her fate, and that she would find peace only in accepting it. If, in revenge, she were to take a lover, her mother continued, and her husband found out, she would be mercilessly killed. That was the way it was and not otherwise, her mother repeated again and again concerning a woman's plight. Like the future Penelope, Medea was instructed to find fulfillment in some useless tapestry. Medea knew her brother Apsyrtus had been given a slave for his bed when he came of age, and she knew of the games between boys. In a corner of the clearing below her window was a hut of earth and rock where boys and men went to sweat off the dirt of the exercise field. She knew of the heated stones and scraping strigils, of the laurel-scented vapors that invigorated the flesh and stirred the users' senses. When the heat had accomplished its cleansing, the men sat on the smooth boulders outside, talking and making jokes, letting the sun dry their bodies while they wound their wet hair into loose curls with their fingers, and painstakingly twirled rows of ringlets into their pubic bush with a twig. The nudity of boys was everywhere, at the games, swimming in the sea, all of which was forbidden for the eyes of those of her sex, but boys were so careless in covering their bodies, in turning aside from girls while they relieved themselves, hooting with laughter as they pissed lengths that could reach yards, calling each other nasty names when one looked at another's boyhood, names girls were supposed to not understand, it all ending with giggles as the boys dropped their chitons and wandered off, an arm around the neck of his best friend. What they did barely hidden she also did to herself, certain she was the only girl in the universe to stoop so low. Raised in ignorance, she would nevertheless go to Jason with infinitely more knowledge than she was supposed to have, yet in practice ignorant of things her brother had experienced since the first blush of pubic down. How different Aeetes had been when raising Apsyrtus. He had taught him, day by day, year by year, the correct way for a boy to become a man, at times guiding the boy step by step, having him repeat, again and again, the gestures and movements that would save his life in battle.

Boys were so careless in covering their bodies.

She had now betrayed her homeland for a boy who was perhaps preparing to leave her on the beach, at the very last moment, while she watched him sail away, the Fleece stored within the *Argo*. It was the fear, the primal terror of every infant: abandonment.

So Medea returned to the *Argo* and, falling to her knees before Jason, warned him that all was known, and that they must set off immediately. She was right, for at that moment Aeetes stood before his people and told them that if his treacherous daughter were not caught and brought to him for punishment, he would avenge himself on the people himself, and as his son Apsyrtus controlled an army loyal to him, the Colchians listened. The troops set off, led by Aeetes in a chariot whose reins were in the hands of Apsyrtus, the king holding aloft a torch of pinewood to light the way. Jason too had set off, and it was at the mouth of the river Phasis that the two forces came into contact, just as the *Argo* made its escape into the choppy waters of the sea. Aeetes ordered his own ships launched, under Apsyrtus, again warning his people that they would pay the price of their very lives should Medea not be brought before him in chains. There was no question of her coming back dead, as it was he who wished to decapitate her with his own hands. Apollonius informs us that the Colchian armada was like an endless flock of birds, as countless as the waves of the sea, and as mad for revenge as a winter blizzard.

The Colchian ships, hundred against one, blocked the entrance to the Hellespont and obliged Jason into negotiations. Apsyrtus could have captured them all, but he was certain that his sister would either be killed in the battle or that she would take her life, and he did not dare face his father with her corpse. Medea went to Jason and again fell to her knees, pleading for his support, as she had given him aid in overcoming the fierce bulls and the dragon, the guardian of the Golden Fleece. She reminded him of his promise to marry her, and hinted of her disgrace should she be caught, for she had surrendered her virginity to the lad, and her father would cut off her head, a head impaired because it was witness to her out-of-marriage depravity. It was this thought that seemed to handicap her most, that she would go before her father, her hymen no long intact, somehow unworthy before this man who had forced innumerous hymens of his own. Her arms clinging to his knees, she said she was not only Jason's wife, but also his sister and daughter. And it was true that in a world of men she had no choice but to plead, as even the air she breathed depended on the generosity of the men about her.

Yet, behind her pleas, there were coals of incandescent fire. For the first time in her life she began to envisage vengeance of her own. Should this man fail her, she dared imagine subtle ways to make him pay, a dagger to the throat as he slept, poisoned wine as he banqueted with friends, seeds that would germinate over the coming years. She went so far as to tell Jason that if he left her stranded she would set the *Argo* afire, destroying the Argonauts; she would gain back her own purity by throwing herself into the flames. Jason saw the rage in her eyes and thought it wise to reassure her, careful, nonetheless, to assert his virility, never allowing himself, as Idas had put it, ''to pay court to girls and their silly heads.''

But Medea had a plan to offer him. Since her brother Apsyrtus wanted talks, Medea would meet with him. She would send him gifts to lesson his caution, one of which was a chiton that had been worn by Dionysus, woven by the divine Graces themselves, scented still with the ambrosial perfume the god wore to seduce Minos' daughter Ariadne, the same who would give herself to Theseus after he destroyed the Minotaur. When Jason agreed, she sent word to Apsyrtus that she had been obliged to help the Argonauts, but that she would now help Apsyrtus regain the Golden Fleece and later, she promised, she would lay her case before her father Aeetes so that he could judge her in the plentitude of his wisdom.

Apsyrtus took the bait and, wearing the god's chiton, presented himself in the splendor of his youth, before his sister, satisfied in the knowledge that his companions were hidden and ready for action should Medea show signs of further treason. As she stood in a clearing outside the temple of Hera, Apsyrtus appeared as if by magic from the surrounding woods. He should have been on his guard, poor lad, the moment Medea turned her back on him, afraid to see the blood of the boy who had grown to manhood at her side, even if the worlds of their youths had been so different they might have grown up on differing continents, his privileged, hers in the service of those whose chitons covered the scepter of their power. Apsyrtus reveled in her fear and in his force, and in a prideful jerk his handsome head threw back this comely black hair, fully revealing the swarthy bronze of his smiling face, a smile that turned to horror as he felt Jason's sword pierce him from behind, while from his chest burst the blade, and blood irrupted that soaked the godly chiton and splattered the robes of his sister. The lad was dead before his knees touched the earth, his torso held suspended until Jason withdrew the sword from the lad's heart, and he fell forward, his face masked by the dust. Jason lopped off his arms and legs and then fell to his knees and, bending over, lapped up the youthful blood that he spat out, three times, the precaution against his being haunted by the boy's eternal ghost. At the same moment the Astronauts fell on Apsyrtus' men, themselves hidden in ambush, and massacred them all. This was Apsyrtus' personal guard, the main of the troops still on his ships.

The *Argo* shoved off, followed by Colchian vessels. To slow them down Jason dispersed Apsyrtus' limbs into the waves. The vessels immediately halted to collect the pieces of flesh and bone, for they were aware of the punishment they would receive at the hands of Aeetes if they failed to do so. The boy had been the king's unique treasure and his only son. Now he was dead as was Aeetes too, for what did he have left now that his dear boy had been taken beyond, far beyond, his loving reach?

Jason and Medea headed back to the Hellespont, back from where they had come, stopping only long enough for Circe, Medea's aunt, to cleanse them both of blood guilt. Circe found Medea's disobedience towards her father and the killing of her own flesh and blood intolerable, as well as her having given herself to a foreigner, and not to one of her own. But Circe herself was far from spotless. Known for her magic spells, she had been so ill treated by men that when sailors landed on her island she invited them to a sumptuous dinner she drugged, turning them, afterwards, into hogs. She had hundreds when Medea and Jason passed through, and thousands years later when Odysseus returned from having destroyed

Troy. Odysseus and his men too landed on the island in search of food. She turned the search party Odysseus had sent out into hogs, and when Odysseus came near her cave in quest of them, she invited him to a meal that he only pretended to eat. When she waved her wand to change him into a hog, he grabbed her by the throat and would have rung her neck had she not promised to change the sailors back into men again, and open her bed for clever Odysseus. He stayed the time needed to produce three sons.

This time the Argonauts went through the Hellespont in the light of day, no longer fearing Troy, for Heracles had passed through the town and had, as already mentioned, slaughtered men and taken women and children as slaves, naming Priam king over the smoldering remains. But as the reader knows, Troy would rise Phoenix-like from its ashes to inspire the greatest of all poets, Homer, to write the greatest of all epics, the *Iliad*.

The *Argo* set sail in the direction of Corcyra. Hera knew that they would have to pass through a narrow channel between two monsters, Charybdis and Scylla, facing each other across what is today the Straits of Messina. Scylla had been the mistress of Poseidon whose wife Amphitrite changed her into a monster with six heads and twelve feet. She seized sailors, cracked their bones and then ate them. Charybdis was an enormous whirlpool. So Hera sent Thetis, Peleus' wife, to instruct him on how to make safe passage through the channel. Peleus and Thetis had lived happily until the birth of Achilles, he who was destined to be greater than his father, the reason Zeus decided not to sleep with Thetis. One night Peleus came upon Thetis who was holding Achilles over a fire, burning away his mortal parts. She had succeeded in destroying everything except the heel of one foot by which she was holding him. Peleus snatched away the boy and Thetis, furious, left him, never to return. Now she sat at Jason's side as he rowed the *Argo*. She informed him of her mission, thanks to which no one on the *Argo* was harmed when passing through the straits. Years later, however, six of Odysseus' men were snatched by Scylla and devoured. Following the passage the crew of the *Argo* beached the boat and had a banquet in thanks of their survival, after which they passed the night in their accustomed way, alongside their accustomed mate.

The *Argo* landed in Corcyra, then named Drepane, today's Corfu. Jason was welcomed by King Alcinous and Medea by his queen Arete. Now, Medea fell to her knees before the queen and begged her help, certain that her father Aeetes had ships on the sea in her search, in which she was right. She didn't need to convince the queen about how shabbily she had been treated in Colchis because outside of Sparta--where women were taught how to fight and were well-fed in order for them to take command of the city should Sparta's two kings ever be absent at the same time--women knew only child bearing and kitchen duty. Queen Arete fought an uphill battle for the rights of women, never hesitating to disturb her husband's sleep with her demands. That night it was in favor of Medea that she kept him from the peaceful arms of life-resituating Morpheus, harassing him with the girl's suffering. Now, a word to you boys: Slumber alongside a lad will never be interrupted by his defending this or that cause, or by reminders to put out the dogs or bring in the milk, and with the exception of rent-boys, you'll never be annoyed by perfume-store gossip and how such and such lightens his hair with gold dust, and so and so has the cheeks of his ass shaved to prolong the aspect of youth. Your only concern will be the ardor of your friend, especially if the lad is but a boy: The poet Tibullus tells us that we have no chance against tender youths, who give us ample reason to love them. This boy is pleasing due to the masterly control he has over his horse; this other one causes our hearts to flutter when he breaks the surface of the water, showing his snow-white chest and nipples; so and so captures us by his daring; such and such by his peaches-and-cream complexion. At times youths objected for the form when men made advances, even menacing to tell their fathers if the men didn't cease. But once bridled, and the man could find rest after expulsing his lust, it was the boy who sought more, awaking the man from sleep by the gentle entreating of his buttocks. Again satisfied, man and boy plunged back into the arms of Sleep for an hour before the boy asked if the man would like to do it again. The man would, but when the boy stirred once more, an hour later, it was the man who threatened the boy, ''If you don't stop I'll tell your daddy!''

(3)

At any rate, after a sleepless night King Alcinous was obliged to come to a decision, as a boat from Colchis, demanding Medea's return, had anchored before his palace at dawn. The king decided that Medea would be sent home if she were still a virgin, if not she would remain with her husband, as was only proper. Queen Arete had gotten wind of what the king had decided and had informed Jason and Medea who arranged to exchange vows before the temple of Hera and who then coupled, in view of palace servants, on a couch covered by the Golden Fleece itself, for the umpteenth time since they'd first met. King Areetes of Colchis was apoplectic when news of his daughter's successful escape reached him a year later, and dropped dead. As for the Colchians sent to retrieve Medea, all but the hardiest fled to other lands for fear of being executed by Aeetes whose death they ignored.

The *Argo* left Corcyra in direction of Iolcus, pausing before the Ile of the Sirens whose sweet music caused many a ship to be drawn to its shoals where they were torn apart and the crews drowned. Thanks to Orpheus' wondrous lyre, which played more beautiful music than the Sirens' sweet songs, the *Argo* passed unhindered. Only handsome Butes opted for the

Siren's charms and jumped overboard. Aphrodite intercepted the lad and would later bear his child. Although she had married the ugliest and most malformed of the gods, Hephaestus, Aphrodite craved beautiful boys, among them Dionysus with whom she had Priapus, a boy of miraculous dimensions who presided over Dionysian orgies, the size and rigor of his tool inspiring both sexes with the lust that fueled their love making. Now she used Butes in order to make Adonis jealous, which worked as Adonis would father two of her children. Adonis' mother was Smyrna who boasted that she was more beautiful than Aphrodite herself. The goddess avenged her honor by making Smyrna's father ravish Smyrna when drunk. Aphrodite had taken Adonis to bed the moment he was old enough to be operative, which enraged Ares, Aphrodite's foremost lover, who sent a boar to fatally gore the lad when he was out hunting. Aphrodite begged Zeus to immortalize the boy, as he had done Ganymede, and like Ganymede, Adonis became Aphrodite's toy-boy from then on.

The *Argo* sailed on to Crete where the love of boys had been celebrated since the island's first great king, Minos. The rites of passage were singular: There a boy was abducted by a lover who, in concord with the boy's friends, takes the lad into the countryside where they spend two idyllic months hunting, feasting and exhausting their young bodies. The belovèd is then returned home with the symbolic gifts of military dress, an ox and a drinking cup, and whatever else the man might wish him to have, gifts the expense of which would depend on the man's resources. Interestingly, the boy was then known by a Greek word meaning "he who stands ready," perhaps signifying Ganymede who, after being abducted by Zeus, stood ready, at the god's side, to serve him food and drink. It's interesting too to note that the boy's father was kept informed of each stage of his son's abduction and, indeed, his great wish was to have a son who would be handsome enough to attract a suitable suitor--one influential enough to give the boy a boost into the better classes, knowing full well that his boy would be the object of sexual passion, as the father had himself been as a boy. (3)

On Crete the crew offered a sacrifice to Zeus, but as they had nothing other than water, it was that they chose to sprinkle on the flaming logs. Jason and Medea were off sporting in the *Argo* and Medea's maids took the occasion to go ashore where they found the boys. When the girls saw that the offering was nothing more than water, they mocked them, their way of careless flirting, but the lads, aware of what their leader was in the midst of enjoying, took the maidens in hand and flirted in their manner, the stretching out of their chitons leaving no doubt as to what they had in mind. Pleasantries led to stolen kisses, fingers innocently brushing healthy breasts while the maidens, who dared, stroked the engorged manhood through the wispy tissue. Soon all were enamored in the way of Jason and Medea, in a quiet disturbed by sighs only, as the men took their fill and then, since they were young, covered the girls passed to them by their belovèds, lusting in the scent of the sweat of the boy the girl had just left, thrilled in the knowledge that that night, under the cover of dark, the boy whose sweat he inhaled would again be his.

It was in the autumn that the *Argo* regained the Iolcus beach of Pagasae, in Thessaly, surrounded by mountains, rich in pastures and sheep, birthplace of Deucalion, the first builder of cities and temples, son of Prometheus, creator of Man.

It is here that Apollonius of Rhodes tells us, in the last sentence of his book, that it was ''with joyful hearts that they stepped ashore at Pagasae.'' But this, dear reader, was far, far from the case.

In the interim Pelias, falsely informed that Jason was dead, ordered Jason's father and mother murdered. Both begged to be allowed to commit suicide. Aeson chose to drink bull's blood while his wife stabbed herself with a dagger. Despite their advanced ages, they had produced a son, Jason's brother, that Pelias himself held by its tiny feet and dashed its down-covered head against the place's marble floor.

What followed was one of the greatest hoaxes in antique history. Jason, when he heard the news of his family's massacre from a passing fisherman, rounded up his men for a conference. He decided on a frontal attack of the palace but his own brother, Acastus, had a cooler head and proclaimed that the place was so well guarded that they would all perish in the attempt. A heated discussion ensued, brought to an end when Medea--who knew men's ways of putting off the inevitable by idle talk that could go on for hours, if not days and weeks--came forward and promised to reduce the palace to impotence, she and her maidens. Amidst hoots of doubts from the crew who knew, from firsthand, that the maidens were good for pleasure, but who doubted other talents.

Medea used her craft to disguise herself as an old crone and, accompanied by her girls, she made her crippled way to the gates of the fortress, under the startled gaze of the guardians. She claimed to have been sent by Artemis to reward Pelias in person for his superb rule over Iolcus. The king, awakened, ordered their entrance. Accompanied by his daughters, he met the crone in his throne room. In gratitude for his rigorous, benevolent governance, said the crone, Artemis wished to rejuvenate Pelias so that, again young, he would have numerous more years to do good. As proof of her powers, she stripped herself of her disguise, revealing a young maiden.

Pelias was no fool, so Medea had prepared a second magic trick. She asked Pelias to provide her with an old ram whose throat her maidens slit and whose body they carved into pieces. A caldron was brought to the central fire pit where water was brought to ebullition and the pieces of flesh boiled. She then had them reunited into a mass that, in the midst of whirling skirts and robes that hid the scene, was replaced by a tiny baby lamb one of the maidens had hidden against her breast. Convinced, Pelias stretched out over a couch after drinking a magic potion, the same Medea had used on the dragon that had kept watch over the Golden Fleece. Pelias' eyes too were deadened by the narcotic brew. Medea then gave orders for Pelias' daughters to cut him into ribbons that she promptly boiled as she had the ram. The only surprise now was the failure of the stinking morsels to form a new and rejuvenated Pelias!

The next day funeral games were held for Pelias. Euphemus won the chariot race, Polydeuces, naturally, the boxing contest, Meleager the javelin throw, Peleus the wrestling match and Zetes and his brother Calais the short and the long foot races. Jason appointed his brother Acastus the new King of Iolcus. As Medea was now the only heir to Aeetes, she had rule over Corinth because before taking power in Colchis, Aeetes had been King of Corinth and had left his friend Bunos there as his regent.

As stated above, Meleager won the javelin contest, and as we're reliving the destinies of the Argonauts as we go along, here is the perfect place to learn about him. The amazing story of Meleager and his mother began just after his birth when for reasons unknown the Fates warned Althaea, Meleager's mother, that her new-born was destined to die the moment a twig in the fireplace was totally consumed. She immediately withdrew it, doused it with water, and hid it in a chest that she buried. Meleager grew into a fine warrior and the finest javelin thrower in all Hellas.

His father, Oeneus, during his sacrifices to the Olympians, had forgotten one of the minor gods, Artemis, goddess of the Hunt. But to get even, she sent a wild boar of immense dimensions to Oeneus' lands with the purpose of destroying his orchards, vines and crops. The damage was so severe and the boar so indomitable that Oeneus sent a herald throughout all of Hellas in search of brave souls willing to kill the animal, the prize being its tusks and pelt.

As with the *Argo*, from all countries and all towns the bravest youths showed up, some who would later adorn the *Argo* as crewmembers. There were the Dioscuri, Castor and Polydeuces; Idas and Lynceus who would later kill Castor and be killed by Polydeuces; plus Jason himself and Admetus. Now, Admetus was the friendly kind of guy the gods appreciated because he was honest and a fair-dealer, and he always had girls on hand for some of the gods, boys for others like Apollo. He decided to marry a beauty named Alcestis and during the marriage ceremony made all the proper sacrifices, except he too forgot Artemis. That night, entering the bridal chamber, certain to find the virginal Alcestis naked, oiled and spread out over his bed, he came upon a nest of serpents. He ran off to Apollo's temple for help. As Apollo, Artemis' brother, had a special liking for Admetus, he went to Artemis and said something like, "Ah shucks Sis, it's his wedding night and the guy wants a little nooky!" The *very* virginal Artemis was only half amused by her beloved brother, but nonetheless amused, as she allowed Admetus access to the virginal Alcestis, and the sheath of a virgin is a unique joy, known but once to every girl, except for Aphrodite who can restore hers just by bathing off the coast of Paphos. Anyway, when Admetus' time on earth was near its end, the gods who, as I said, really did like him, promised he could live on if someone would take his place. Admetus therefore went to his parents, old and near the end of their own allotted time, and begged one of them to please die. Both refused. There must be a lesson somewhere in that, but I'll leave it to the reader to find. Then a *coup de théâtre*. His wife Alcestis took poison so he could live on. But in Hades Persephone, tired of the excesses women went through for their men, washed out her stomach and sent her back. Admetus, like all of us, sooner or later, had to face the music alone, just like us all. But before that fatal moment, he had gone boar hunting, where we now find him.

Nestor of sandy Pylos was there at the boar hunt too. He was a young lad then, handsome and another of Heracles' endless paramours. He had been, Pausanius tells us, more loved by Heracles than even Iolaus or Hylas, whom he lost to water nymphs. It was Heracles who gave Pylos to Nestor to rule, after having killed Nestor's father King Neleus. One wonders how Nestor felt, later on, when reunited with Heracles, and found him in the arms of still another lad.

Peleus was present for the boar hunt, as was Eurytion. Now, Peleus and Eurytion, whom Peleus would later that day accidentally kill, had been lovers when Peleus came to the court of Eurytion's father King Actor to be cleansed for having killed his brother Phocus. Phocus was the youngest son of King Aeacus, and King Aeacus was the father of Peleus and Telamon. Both Peleus and Telamon felt in danger of losing their father's kingdom when Aeacus, due to his immoderate love for his son Phocis, gave him rule over neighboring lands. Phocis' brothers decided to kill him, but the murder had to be presented as an accident if they wished to escape their father's rage. They challenged the boy to an athletic contest during which a stone discus accidently-on-purpose struck the lad's head, immediately felling him. As Phocis was only stunned, Peleus came up from behind and split the beautiful head in two with his axe. As stated, Peleus went to King Actor to be washed clean of bloodguilt, where he met the king's son Eurytion.

Telamon was present for the boar hunt as was Caeneus. Now, Caeneus was the world's very first transsexual. He had been born a girl, for whom Poseidon had an irresistible attraction. They met and mated, and in thanks

Poseidon asked her what he could offer in exchange for the felicity she had given him. Caeneus said she wanted a man's power and pleaded with Poseidon to give her a man's scepter. This Poseidon did, so successfully that Caeneus, now a boy, produced a son, Coronus (alas, later killed by Heracles). Poseidon named him King of the Lapiths, and now Caeneus--the warrior he had always wished to be--was at Oeneus' Palace, prepared to win the boar's pelt.

Ancaeus and Cepheus were there too, impatiently stomping the ground in their haste to kill the boar. Later Perseus would turn Cepheus to stone for his refusal to give him his daughter, and the fate of Ancaeus, as we shall see, is every man's worst nightmare.

This is the story of Perseus: Acrisius, King of Argos, wanted a son and consulted the Delphic Oracle who told him that his *daughter* would have a boy, but that the boy would grow up and kill Acrisius. So Acrisius locked away his daughter who was nonetheless impregnated by Zeus who took the form of a golden shower. The son she bore was Perseus. Acrisius refused to kill them both so instead locked them in a chest that he flung into the sea. The chest was netted by fishermen loyal to King Polydectes who reared Perseus. Polydectes wanted to marry Perseus' mother but Perseus refused him her hand, telling the king he would give him whatever else he wanted. The king said he would settle for the Gorgon Medusa, a monster having a terrible face and hair of serpents, a face so horrible that the person looking on it froze with fright. The gods favored Perseus and gave him a sack in which to put the head, winged feet to get to it, a sickle to cut it off, and the helmet of invisibility belonging to Hades. Perseus collected the head and returned (after profuse adventures) to Polydectes who said he had sent the boy away to be killed by the Medusa, and had never planned to give up his mother. Perseus opened the sack, looked the other way, and froze Polydectes to stone. He then returned to Argos where, during Olympic-style games, he threw a discus that rebounded and killed Acrisius.

For nine days the men made merry before the boar hunt. Oeneus supplied them with tables laden with food, and servers, boys and girls, imminently susceptible to disappearing with the men to their rooms, until the wine had done its job and they all gave themselves to group sport in a Dionysian spree that spanned the whole night. Only Atalanta took no part.

Now, Atalanta's father had wanted a son so badly that he couldn't face the fact that this was not so when at birth the child had been brought before him, laid at his feet, and the baby robe parted so he could see the wished-for scepter. Normally in such cases, the father would pick up a son and hold him over his head, to the cheers of his subjects. But if it were a girl, he would simple issue the order: ''Let it eat!'' In this case he was so disappointed that he shouted, ''Have it exposed!''

Atalanta was taken to a dump outside the city walls and left to die. Dumps were well-known sites for such acts, and farmers occasionally passed by in hopes of finding free labor as the child grew. Atalanta was lucky in being found by hunters who taught her to shoot arrows as proficiently as Artemis herself and, astonishingly, they honored her virginity.

Meleager took part in the nightly orgies, although this was but a physical need, as his heart belonged to Atalanta. But Meleager's mother's brothers didn't want a woman in domains reserved for men, and refused to accept her among them. Meleager declared that without Atalanta he would withdraw from the hunt and would make sure that the majority of the other men did likewise. Oeneus chose to let her take part.

The men entered the surrounding woods in a half-moon arc but even before flushing out the boar there was trouble. Two centaurs were present and as they'd had access to wine, they'd become mad with lust, and the easiest prey appeared to be Atalanta, whom both tried to straddle. But for the girl these two, Hylaeus and Rhaecus by name, represented hardly a break in her stride. She brought down both with an arrow to the heart.

The boar finished by springing from its hideaway and immediately killed two men, frightening young, handsome Nestor so badly that he climbed up a tree and stayed there. Jason missed with his javelin but Iphicles grazed it with his spear. Telamon stepped forward to stick the beast with his sword but was tripped by a root. His brother Peleus went to right him but the boar, aware of their vulnerability, turned to kill them both. Luckily it swerved from its trajectory thanks to Atalanta who shot it with an arrow just behind the ear, an arrow that bounced off the thick hide. Ancaeus sneered at her and bellowed out, "Let a *man* do the job!" and swung at the boar with his axe. The swing was wide and the boar turned and not only disemboweled Ancaeus with one horn, but turned its head so the other horn could rip away the totality of what made Ancaeus the man he had been so proud of flouting.

In the chaos Peleus killed his friend and former lover Eurytion with a javelin throw meant for the boar, but Eurytion had jumped in the way of the flying missile. The animal chose Theseus for its target but Meleager stopped it with a spear to the flank, followed by his sword that he thrust into its heart.

The men surrounded the boar, kicking it with their bare feet. Meleager could have had servants cut away the pelt but he did it himself so he could offer it, still steaming and bloody, to Atalanta, saying it was hers because she had drawn first blood and, anyway, her arrow would have eventually brought it down, which was blatantly false.

Here the two men who had stormed at Atalanta's taking part in the hunt, Meleager's mother's brothers Plexippus and Iphicles, said she in no way deserved the prize because her shot had just been lucky and, anyhow, this was only Meleager's way of sucking up to a silly female. Meleager killed them both with such rapidity they had only time to show astonishment, both hearts pierced by his sword, still wet with the boar's gore.

Meleager's mother, watching the bodies of her two brothers being carried off the field, decided the cruelest and most incomprehensible act a parent can submit its child to, she disinterred the twig she had buried, she took it to her fireplace and lit it, thusly ending the life she had brought into this world.

As for Atalanta, there were many destinies allotted to her by historians, none deserving replay here.

We last left Jason and Medea in Iolcus where Medea had cut King Pelias into pieces and Jason had turned over the throne to his brother. Jason and Medea then went off to settle in Corinth, which was part of her inheritance. There they lived happily, Madea producing fourteen children, seven boys and seven girls, in just over ten years. Then Jason's roving eye fell on the young Glauce, daughter of the King of Creon. As the Corinthians had come to love the gentle rule of Jason, they favored his choice of new bride, as well as his divorce of Medea who had always been to straight-laced for simpler Corinthian tastes.

Medea was forced to agree, and in proof of her good intentions she organized a huge festival in the palace, to which King Creon, his daughter, and all the notables of Corinth and Thebes, Creon's domain, were invited. Following the formula used by Deianeira, the wife of Heracles, Medea imbibed a wondrous dress she offered Glauce with the blood and semen of a centaur. As Glauce approached the central hearth the dress, as had Heracles' new shirt, burst into flames that enveloped them all except Medea who had stepped away in safety and Jason who dove from the nearest window. Hera then appeared before Medea, in agreement with her that wayward husbands had to be punished--as Hera had repeatedly tried to punish Zeus for his infidelities. Hera also knew that Zeus, impressed by Medea's spunk, had tried to seduce her, but had been turned down flat, another reason for Hera to help the girl. Hera promised Medea that she would make all her children, themselves immolated in the fire, immortal, all but Medeius who was at that moment being educated by Cheiron the Centaur. Hera's promise may or may not have been kept, as from that moment on all of Medea and Jason's children vanished into the mists of History.

Medea went to Athens where she married King Aegeus. Now, Medea and Aegeus went way back, to the time he had had two wives, neither of which produced a son. Medea, aware of her precariousness in the world of her father and brother, divined the goodness in Aegeus and confided her fears. Aegeus promised that should she ever need someone, he would always be there for her. In exchange, Medea offered to help him father a boy. She chose a girl who had no chance of marriage because she had decided to guard her virginity to her death. But Medea had a special powder she had the girl unsuspectingly take in a drink, an infusion that made her wild with lust. The girl had chosen an island as her sanctuary, upon which Aegeus, directed by Medea's protector Hera, shipwrecked. The girl, maddened by the drink, scented his arrival and welcomed him with wild caresses and kisses. When Aegeus had literally nothing more to offer her, she chose to swim across a channel that separated her isle from an isle set aside by Cheiron the Centaur for the boys he taught military strategy and weaponry. While crossing she was impregnated by Poseidon, drawn to the rancid odor of her and Aegeus' bodies. From these two couplings would be born, by-and-by, the great Theseus. The next morning, amidst the bodies of the lads who had shared her, she became aware of her degradation and, free of Medea's potion, went to distant Troezen to give birth. Hera had left a sword and a shield by her side that she took with her for protection from men she once again feared. These weapons she later gave her boy, Theseus. At age 16 he offered his first hair cutting to Apollo at Delphi, a moment of extreme importance in the life of a lad, one tenderly appreciated by the god.

After the events described above had taken place, Medea, having burned her palace at Corinth and everyone in it, fled to Athens where she reminded Aegeus of his promise to shelter her should she be in need. She was well received and as she was still beautiful and had evident knowledge of powders and spells, something that could always come in handy, Aegeus married her.

Theseus, eager to discover the world, left Troezen and headed for the great capital, Athens, where, thanks to her powers, Medea immediately recognized him as the boy birthed thanks to her intervention. But now that she had a home and loving husband, she wanted nothing to disturb her tranquility, she who had known such terrible ups-and-downs, escaping a murderous father and tyrannical brother, offering fourteen babies to the man she adored but who left her, the reason for the holocaust she had been responsible for. She presented the lad to Aegeus and convinced him that Theseus was a treacherous spy set to overthrow Aegeus' rule. Because Aegeus had no idea who could have sent him, he decided to act with circumspection, welcoming the boy while planning his accidental demise. Theseus was invited to a banquet where Medea surreptitiously slipped the king a drink of wolfsbane, a deadly poison, he himself was to present to the boy. This Aegeus did, giving him his cup, all the while admiring his wondrous body, the squared-off pectorals, the magnificent biceps as Theseus drew the drink to his lips, the handsome fleece of auburn hairs that descended from the navel to the leather strap that held his sword in place. Recognizing the handle of the sword, Aegeus had just time enough to slap the cup away, before asking its provenance.

What took place next was a series of festivities Athens and Athenians had never known before, or even imagined possible. Aegeus was, at last, a father, a father of the most beautiful boy to have walked the earth. His lust for the boy changed to fatherly admiration, and it was announced to all that it was Theseus Aegeus' successor. Medea fled Athens when Aegeus became aware of her treachery.

After the departure of Medea from Athens, the ninth year of a very special cycle came around. This is its story: A wild bull had brought havoc to the vicinity of Marathon, destroying crops and killing anyone who tried to stop it. One of those gored to death was the son of Minos, the great King of Crete. In recompense for the death of his boy, Minos demanded that Athens, every nine years, surrender seven of its most beautiful girls and seven of its most handsome lads, to be enjoyed by Minos himself until he tired of them, after which they were given to the Minotaur, who did with them as he wished. Now, the genesis of the Minotaur is of x-rated libertinage. It began with Zeus whose love for Europa produced three sons, Minos, Sarpedon and Rhadamanthys, after which Zeus married Europa off to Asterius, King of Crete, who adopted the boys. All three sons fell madly in love with Miletus, a wondrously beautiful lad, who chose Sarpendon to warm his bed, before emigrating to Phrygia where he founded the great city of Miletus. On his adopted father's death, Minos became King of Crete. He took Pasiphaë for wife, and in celebration asked Poseidon to provide a bull that Minos would sacrifice in honor of Poseidon himself. The god did as requested but the bull, snow-white, was of such beauty that Minos sacrificed another in its place. This so angered Poseidon that he made Pasiphaë fall madly in love with the beast. She asked the palace craftsman, Daedalus, to do what was necessary so that she could be covered by the white animal. Daedalus crafted a cow, hollow so that Pasiphaë could slip into her interior. It was thus that Daedalus led the bull to his creation and watched it engage its enormous engine into the slot that led into Pasiphaë's cunt, affording her more pleasure than she conceived possible. The outcome of this monstrous coupling was the Minotaur, whose head was that of a beast, his body that of a man.

Pasiphaë, Daedalus, the cow.

Disgusted by these events, Minos turned to the Oracle of Delphi for advice. The Oracle instructed him to have Daedalus build a labyrinth in Minos' palace at Knossos, wherein he would hide both Pasiphaë and the child she would soon give birth to. This he did, providing the Minotaur, every nine years, with the boys and girls from Athens, after Minos himself had made use of them. He imprisoned Daedalus on the island for his role in Pasiphaë's perversion, but Daedalus cleverly constructed wings for himself and his dear son, Icarus, wings they used to escape to neighboring Naxos. On the way the boy, exuberant to find himself flying over unknown lands and unexplored waters, swooped low and flew high. Daedalus warned him that he would waterlog the wings if he approached the sea too closely, and he would melt the wax that held the feathers together if he flew too near the sun. But boys are boys, as the reader knows, and such has been and will always be true, to the immense pleasure of we who love them. But in this case Icarus flew too high, the wax melted, and he fell into the sea and drowned, from which place rose the Isle of Icaria, visible on a clear day from beautiful Myconos. Daedalus continued on to Sicily where he entertained the Sicilian court with his inventions. Minos, however, came to capture him. He too was well received and offered a banquet, before which he was permitted to bathe. But the king's family, aware that Minos was there only to recapture Daedalus, had Daedalus pierce the ceiling of the bath, and while Minos enjoyed the warm pool Daedalus poured boiling water on him, scalding him to death. Zeus named Minos judge of the dead in Tartarus and had his brother Rhadamanthys replace him on the throne of Crete.

Pasiphaë's baby, the Minotaur.

But for the moment Theseus is in Athens, preparing to destroy the Minotaur. He decided to put an end to the nine-year cycle by going to Crete himself, accompanied by six other boys and seven effeminate lads made up as girls, who were ordered to smoothen their skin with oils and avoid the bronzing sun. They learned to talk and walk like girls, to smother themselves in perfume, to the great pleasure of their buddies who were quick to take advantage of the confusion of the sexes by pleasing them where--or nearly where--girls receive *their* pleasure.

They caste off from the Piraeus, the ship adorned with black sails as was the custom, but Theseus promised his father Aegeus that they would return with white sails, proof of their victory over Minos.

On arrival Minos immediately made off with one of the "girls" and Theseus made the acquaintance of Minos' daughter Ariadne, equally eager to honor the handsome lad. Afterwards, she provided Theseus with a ball of string that he was to unwind as he made his way through the labyrinth, the only means for him to find his way back. What happened in the depths of the Minotaur's domain is unknown. Some say Theseus found the Minotaur asleep and plunged his sword into its chest, others that there had been a prolonged fight, but in the end Theseus made his way back to the light, his bloody sword proof of his triumph. He rounded up the Athenian boys and fled to neighboring Naxos with Ariadne where all concerned enjoyed a welcomed layover. Why Theseus left the island without Ariadne is not known, other than his wish to be unhampered in his future conquests. Dionysus reigned over Naxos and, averted of Ariadne's presence on his island by her sobs, comforted her in godly fashion before finally marrying the lass.

Theseus returned home but he had forgotten to change the black sails for white ones. Aegeus saw the ship's arrival from afar, on the top of the cliffs of Sounion. Unable to face the loss of his boy, he threw himself into the sea, known as the Aegean from then on.

As Aegeus' wife Pasiphaë was the daughter of Helios, she was immortal. She didn't die but she did waste away into a very old and wrinkled crone.

Alas, the end of Theseus was highly unworthy of such a man. As no one of mark had visited his island of Scyros since Thetis and her son Achilles had left, Lycomedes was thrilled to welcome Theseus whom he thought was just passing through. But Theseus had lands on Scyros, and the point of his visit was to recuperate them and put them on a paying basis, thanks to fields of olive trees that he planned to turn over to a friend who would act as his regent, lands that Lycomedes had long since annexed as his own. Once Theseus' intentions became clear, Lycomedes invited him to his palace on the summit of a cliff facing the sea, and after putting Theseus at ease with stories of Thetis and her seducing ways, he simply pushed him over the edge as he learned to see something Lycomedes was pointing out to him.

The apotheosis of Jason, too, was sad indeed. The goddesses, led by Hera who greatly favored Medea, turned their backs on the youth and his fornicating ways, and where once Destiny had smiled on him, now he knew only demeaning age and solitude as he lost his precious beauty. Years passed, many, many years, at the conclusion of which he decided to seek the shelter of the only veritable happiness he had known, his wondrous *Argo*, beached but still as solid as a rock, thanks to Athena's hand in its construction. Under its powerful prow, a beam with oracular talents and as strong as a girder of steel, he sat and remembered the events of the past, and especially the loves he had known among the young, valiant Argonauts, all of which had played out, on distant beaches, in sight of this very prow. But in the Heavens Clotho was spinning the thread of life that Lachesis measured and Atropos cut when it came to its conclusion, and no hand could still their labor. When the extremity of Jason's own thread approached the shears they signaled to Athena, dear to vengeful Hera, who allowed the prow to fall in one shift blow upon Jason below. His last thoughts may have been of himself in the arms of a vibrant youth, the wondrous end that we, who love Jason, know to be more precious than all the adventures in the world.

For the pleasure of the eyes - 1

FERDINAND MAGELLAN
And His Flagship the Trinidad
1480 – 1521

Ignorance and superstition took a huge hit when Ferdinand Magellan's crew circumnavigated the world, proving it was not flat. The forces that push some men to do what they do are truly mindboggling, and both Alexander VI and Magellan possessed those forces. In 1494 Alexander VI divided the world in two parts, West of a line that divided the Atlantic down the middle went to Spain, the East went to Portugal. Alexander got the king of Spain to agree to the division and, while he was at it, he gave King Ferdinand and Queen Isabella permission to initiate the Inquisition and rid Spain of Jews and Moors (it must be remembered that Alexander, a Borgia, was himself Spanish). Magellan was a totally fearless warrior, many times wounded in battles against the Arabs. Magellan set out from Seville to discover a route to the Spice Islands, the source of spices that, at the time, far outweighed gold in value. He was given five ships--all totally black due to the pitch that covered even the masts--and 260 sailors, for the most part illiterate scum who thought only of their stomachs and scrotums. They sailed first to the Canary Islands and then to Brazil. During the trip a sailor was caught sodomizing a page. Pages, aged eight to fifteen, were shanghaied to do the menial jobs onboard. The general rule at sea was simply to look away when one was caught in a sex act, the norm being that sailors, in their teens and twenties, took care of each other's carnal needs. For some unknown reason Magellan took offense now, perhaps because the boy was very young. The sailor was garroted (a rope encircled his throat and a stick--called garrote in Spanish--was introduced between the neck and rope and turned until the man was strangled to death). What happened to the lad is unclear. Either he jumped overboard or was thrown; at any rate, he too died. On the coast of Brazil the sailors enjoyed accepted sex with native women, the price being a nail or any other metal object. The crewmembers were careful not to venture far from the ships, as they knew that the natives practiced cannibalism and human sacrifices. The men suffered terribly from heat in summer, as well as from rats and mice that left feces and urine in their food, and lice, bedbugs and cockroaches.

The Straits of Magellan were called, at the time, the Dragon's Tail due to their incredible complexity. To find the passage Magellan had to investigate countless dead ends. Then winter set in. At this latitude winters were terrible: blizzards, storms, howling winds and cold so intense it was a wonder any of them survived. Magellan put the crew on half rations and because no one really believed that a passage existed and because Magellan was inflexible and unfeeling, mutiny was in the air. The first mutiny was foiled because a few crew members, loyal to Magellan, managed to trick the mutiny leader into thinking they were on his side, giving them the opportunity to grab him by the beard and plunge a dagger into both his throat and head. A priest who had taken part in the revolt was abandoned, in the snow, on an island. Other traitors were mercilessly beaten but not killed as they were needed to run the ships. A few days later, under the cover of night, another ship mutinied by setting a course back to Spain. During my research I discovered an incredible quirk that existed at the time. Saints were listed as being veritable members of the crew. For example, Santo Antonio because he was known to rescue ships; Santa Barbara because she calmed storms. More incredible still, they received a percentage of the profits when the ships returned to port, profits that were turned over to the church.

When Magellan exited the straits he is said to have cried for joy. He was now in the Pacific, a stretch of water, in his mind, less in width than the Atlantic. He would discover that, in reality, it covered half the world, and he was already nearly out of food. Thanks to the Trade Winds, they made it to Guam three months later, although many men were dead from scurvy. They reached Cebu several months after that. Here Magellan became blood brothers with the Prince, both of whom mingled their blood in a bowl mixed with wine that they drank. Ravishing young girls were offered, virgins who had their vaginas enlarged from birth in order to accommodate men who inserted gold bolts through their penises, just under the glans. The tube of the bolts had a hole through which urine passed. The bolted penises were difficult to insert and they didn't allow rapid movements, meaning that intercourse lasted a very long time, even an entire day, and the men could pull out only when soft. The women claimed the bolts gave them ultimate pleasure.

So friendly was Magellan with the Prince that he offered to wage the Prince's battles for him, certain of his superiority thanks to firearms. All the Prince had to do was convert to Christianity, which he did, along with 2,500 of his subjects. Magellan went after those who didn't, so numerous that their poisoned arrows and spears, aimed at the crew's unarmored legs, proved fatal to Magellan and many others.

One ship made it back to Spain, three years after having left, its sails and rigging rotting. Of the original 260 only 18 men had survived, among them the ship's greatest treasure, Antonio Pigafetta, an historian who gave us such a detailed account of the voyage that books, based on his observations, have been published, from the time of his arrival to our own day.

Magellan

For the pleasure of the eyes – 2

THE TRIAL OF EDWARD RIGBY 1698

Of far greater interest to us than the homosexuality of Captain Edward Rigby of the *Dragon*, a 40-gun man-of-war, was what he saw during a visit from Peter the Great, a boy-king who had gone to the Netherlands to learn how to build and sail boats, his adoration of the Dutch such that he adopted their flag as his own, simply reversing the colors. It's inexact to say the Peter was bisexual because at the time men took their pleasure with both sexes, and that since the ancient Greeks. In this case Rigby was a part of those welcoming Peter, who saw the king fucking his favorite, Alexander Menshikov, through a keyhole, and used the fact to convince a boy he lusted for, 19-year-old William Minton, to allow him to do what Peter had done to Menshikov.

Nearly as interesting as Peter himself, Menshikov had sold buns on the streets of Moscow when one of Peter's favorites took the handsome lad into his service, later handing him over to Peter who made him his next favorite, and that until his death. Menshikov was a master thief who built a magnificent palace for himself, and during one period literally ran Russia for two years during the absence of Peter. Peter, spurred on by continuous complaints about Menshikov's theft of unheard-of sums, finally decided to discharge him. But the lad fell nearly fatally ill, after which Peter forgave all. At Peter's death Menshikov was vital in placing Catherine on the throne, where he reigned supreme until her death, after which he strove to be the power behind the throne of Prince Peter II, perhaps envisioning a *coup-d'état*, but at any rate he planned to marry his daughter to Peter. Overturned by court nobles, he was banished to Siberia where both his wife and daughter died, as he eventually did himself.

As for Rigby, he had seen Minton in Saint James's Park and had apparently quite directly introduced his hand into the boy's trousers while kissing him and forcing the boy's hand down his own pants where, the boy later told the police, the instrument was rock hard. The police set up a sting operation in a hotel where Rigby had invited the boy the next day. They took an adjoining room and told Minton to call out ''Westminster'' once he'd gotten Rigby in a compromising position, which wasn't difficult as Rigby pushed himself against the lad's buttocks, immediately discharging in his own trousers, although he assured the boy that he was still randy enough to fuck him. It was then he revealed having caught Peter and Menshikov in love's embrace on a ship in the Netherlands. He pushed Minton into a corner where he ''pulled down *Mintons* Breeches, turn'd away his shirt, put his Finger to *Mintons* Fundament, and applyed his Body close to Mintons, who feeling something warm touch his Skin, put his hand behind him, and took hold of Rigbys Privy Member, and said to Rigby 'I have now discovered your base Inclinations, I will expose you to the World, to put a stop to these Crimes'; and thereupon Minton went towards the door, Rigby stopt him, and drew his Sword, upon which Minton gave a stamp with his foot, and cry'd out '*Westminster*' ".

Found guilty, Rigby was fined £1,000, given a year's imprisonment, and sent to the pillory three times. The pillories, illustrated below, were located in Haymarket. They could hold four men at a time, whose suffering lasted an hour, during which women with baskets of fish guts, rotten eggs, human and animal dung, potatoes, pig blood and dead cats pelted them.

Pillories

When their hour was up they were led away to Newgate Prison-- encrusted with filth, knocked down, kicked and hit with objects on the way, arriving bleeding profusely.

Once freed Rigby fled to France where he captained the French man-of-war *Toulouse* until captured and jailed at Port Mahon. He escaped aboard a Genoese ship in the harbor and made his way back to France where it is said he was highly valued and well paid for his sailing skills, money he used "for his pleasures said to have been expensive," without, alas!, details on what they might have been.

For the pleasure of the eyes – 3

PIERRE ANDRÉ DE SUFFREN
Captain of the *Mignonne*
1729 – 1788

That such a creature as Pierre André de Suffren could have existed in the 1700s in unbelievable. His parents were Italians from Livorno, and had been drawn to France by the popes who had taken shelter from dirty, vulgar and dangerous Rome in sweet Avignon. Like all bourgeois boys, he was farmed out to a wet-nurse until around age 5 and then sent to a boarding school. At around 14 he was admitted into the ranks of the Maritime Guards open to boys of breeding. His natural bent was literature and history, his chief handicap mathematics. Probably never handsome, always slightly tubby, he developed into what his biographers insist was a fat slob, going nearly naked in the tropics, otherwise wearing the minimum, his shirts dirty, the collars filthy. He never bathed more than once a week, if that much, didn't shave when commanding a ship at sea, was said to stink and lived to eat at all hours of the day and night.

His men adored him, even when he kicked them--an act of affection because he at least acknowledged their existence. He cared for their health, an inexistent concern at the times, and encouraged them to live in couples, fucking at will, reasoning that such mores had existed in Sparta and had been the foundation of the Sacred Band, thanks to which lovers and their beloveds fought to the death rather than show cowardliness. He was an expert tactician and no one could navigate a ship better. He never satisfied himself with a good showing against the enemy, but chased his adversary until his ship was literally sunk from under him. Off his ship he shaved, bathed, dressed impeccably because his parents and educators had raised him to be a gentleman, and thanks to his interest in literature, his conversation was brilliant and entertaining. Back on board he allowed those men averse to homosexual friendships to make holes in a barrel, at differing heights, where they could thrust until depositing their ejaculate at the barrel bottom. Thus protected from women who would steal their money and leave them diseased, the sailors were the most mentally and physically well balanced in the fleet. The king and other nobles apparently knew what was going on, their throats hot with derisive laughter, as the French say, but his value as a victorious seaman made him indispensable and, anyway, he was known to compensate for his sodomitic ways by seducing wives who were somehow not put off by his obesity and sweaty smell when in the midst of cuckolding their husbands.

He was stationed in Malta from 1749 to 1754 and became a Knight. Fighting during this period centered around the defeat of pirates and the English who entered Mediterranean waters. At age 27 he was promoted second in command of the *Orphée*. He was stationed at Toulon and navigated between there and Malta in constant hopes of being given his own vessel. Finally he was awarded a frigate of 26 cannon, the *Mignonne* (translated as everything from ''cute'' to ''sweetie''). He sailed to Greece and the Dardanelles. So great was his reputation as a scourge of both the English and pirates that he was offered a command in the Turkish fleet, which he declined.

In 1778 France aligned itself with America in its War of Independence. Suffren came across the English on several occasions and during one battle he found himself highly outnumbered. But as the English were unaware of his presence, he attacked. His victory added to his reputation for bravery to such an extent that the Minister of the Marine requested to meet him. They dined and from then on Suffren's advancement was guaranteed.

His doctors said that although he was feeling low, he decided to visit a friend in Versailles. There his state of health declined enough for King Louis XVI's own doctors to decide to bleed him. The moment the blade touched a vein, he fell into a coma and shortly afterwards died.

Then years later a historian happened on a man who had served under Suffren and said that the Vice-Admiral had been killed in a duel by a certain Mirepoix who had pleaded with Suffren to aid two of his nephews imprisoned for unknown reasons. Suffren refused, there were insults, and finally a duel. The historian swallowed the story and published it.

Then a third plot was advanced by a writer, Pierre Varillon, who wrote that Suffren had been assassinated by the English because they knew that the king was going to name him to head the French Atlantic fleet, which would have assured England's defeat.

Finally, the family of a certain Cillard claimed that Cillard had been captain of the *Sévère* and dismissed by Suffren. He then disappeared a few years before returning to teach Suffren a lesson, which he did by jumping onto his carriage as he left Versailles and knifed him. At the time, supposedly, this version was believe by many in the navy itself.

Someone who cared so much for his men that he was said to have arranged weddings aboard his vessels, especially keen on uniting old sailors and youths, who saw to the food they ate, to the comfort of their hammocks, to their health, to easing the tension in their balls, just couldn't--said those who loved him--have simply died in bed, a mere mortal.

For the pleasure of the eyes - 4

BOYS AT SEA
1750

Taking on cabin boys was a genial way for the Royal Navy to hire and train its future sailors. Officers' sons could be admitted at age 11, age 13 for others. Genial too was the pay scale. The boys were paid at the same rates as a seaman, the officer responsible for them obliged to spend 1/5th of the amount on the boys' clothing and necessities, pocketing the remaining 4/5ths, an incredible incentive to hire the boys as servants. For each crew that consisted of 100 men or more, an admiral was allowed 10 to 16 boys, a captain 4, carpenters, gunners and boatswains (petty officers in charge of the hull and ship equipment) 2 boys, and lieutenants, cooks and surgeons 1 lad each. But strong boys could also be taken on as able seamen, so numerous that some enemy ships, once they surrendered, complained, when taken on the royal ships as prisoners, that they had been conquered by mere children.

As servants the boys escaped impoverishment, crime and learned a trade. Some would wind up officers themselves. Immediately on being taken aboard they were given marine clothes, instantly making them the equal of their peers. A heartrending statistic concerned their height at age 14 (although often taken on at age 13, at stated above, the *legal age* was nonetheless 14): the lads were 4'3" due to malnutrition and adult abuse, while in the general population the height was 5'1". Another extremely sad fact was that most were scarred by smallpox, to such an extent that, in the absence of photos, the forms (patterns) the scarification took were used to describe them. The boys came from the laboring classes, and 50% had no fathers, 1/5th no adult to care for them at all.

The boys' enrolment was voluntary, but many benevolent organizations and good men saw to it that the lads were more or less impressed as a way of saving them from reformatories, a sure route to the apprenticeship of crime and, later, the gallows.

An amazing fact is that all poor boys in England were supposed to be apprenticed to some trade or as servants, their masters responsible for their care: feeding, clothing and education. When this was not the case the parish was held responsible for them, all of which depended on the honesty of the masters responsible for their welfare. (Even in schools for the rich, headmasters pocketed as much of the parents' money as possible, provoking riots and claims, at places like Eton, that the boys were starving [6].) Of course, boys by their very nature are unruly, and in one way or another the very best methods of ridding society of the most unwieldy was by sending them to sea, whether they liked it or not.

Naturally, many did wish to go, to see the world, just like today, for such has been the destiny of lads since the first crossed over from Africa, in discovery of all the continents except Antarctica. Freedom, adventure, restlessness are a boy's heritage, and thankfully so.

The Marine Society of London was responsible for recruiting the lads, and may truly have had their interests at heart. Some boys, like the fictional Robinson Crusoe, did come from the homes of caring parents, and the Marine Society was said to have helped them find their wayward sons who had run away, the use of smallpox scars as an early "fingerprint".

A boy on a ship could learn a great deal from the men around him, and although some men may have been harsh, in the number it is quite likely that the boy found others who would apprentice him, and perhaps offer the love he'd never had from a father. Few places provided a surer road to manhood, and in being apprenticed on land was no certainty at all that a boy's existence would have been easier and free from abuse, as an apprentice cobbler, smithy, tradesman, weaver, tailor or shoemaker may have had more demanding chores than those aboard ships, and serving some petty bourgeois was certainly less colorful than serving the captain of a vessel. As for entry into the clergy, the clothing may have been more refined but a priest's cock in his ass would have soon changed him into a surrogate girl, hardly better off than a eunuch in an ottoman harem. Misuse in such a way may have been par for the course on ships, but there were compensations for those who didn't like it. There was discovery, there were islands, there were girls ashore, because the men were rarely less than omnisexual.

On a ship the boy had constant companions, a true necessity for a boy's growth, regular meals (often maggoty but the men were said to grow used to it), clothing, a bed, and government-assured wages. And in the tradition of Drake, wealth could be theirs through boarding enemy ships (even cabin boys received a tiny percentage of the loot). Discipline on a ship varied from draconian to liberal, often both combined on the same vessel, where men could make love in full view of others (as there were not the limitless nooks and crannies found on modern vessels), but be lashed for stealing a potato.

Off the ship a lad's uniform was the envy of boys tied to the land, their pockets always had a few coppers, the women were plentiful and cheap, and as lads always, *always* drank, taverns were even more plentiful, and if one didn't want a girl, one was always certain to find a mate who would welcome him, especially if he paid for a round of drinks. The flipside was when a man wanted to marry and settle down. How could he amass enough money to establish himself? He couldn't hide it in his cot, especially as ships were known to sink. Who on land could he entrust it to, and how would he recuperate even a farthing if he were shanghaied, as was the case when a ship needed new bodies? In addition to this inconvenience, there were far more accidents on a ship than experienced by a servant serving his master tea; there was exposure to the elements, sickness and disease; as well as wars, storms and shipwrecks. But it was life, an incontestable chunk of real life. (Sincere gratitude to Roland Pietsch, upon whose excellent article, *Ships' Boys and Youth Culture in Eighteenth-Century Britain: The Navy Recruits of the London Marine Society*, the above paragraphs are based.)

Men on ships had long trousers they could role up, and short-waisted jackets worn over heavy kitted jerseys--a wool garment that originated on the island of Jersey--kept them warm. Due to contacts with Polynesia tattoos had become popular, even among the most educated classes like that of Joseph Banks on Cook's voyage, although Banks himself hid his on his buttocks. Those who had tattoos, weather-beaten faces and hands scarred by rope burns, were visible targets for pressgangs. The men on ships were given an average of eight pints of beer and rum per day which helped them face their strenuous work, the alcohol content of which they burned off rapidly. Shore leave took place regularly, allowing the men access to drink and women, for a price. Women were also occasionally allowed on board if the men declared them to be "their wives" to officers stationed at the gangplanks. The expression "shake a leg" comes from the fact that early in the morning men were awoken to begin the day's work, while women sleeping overnight could avoid being roused by shaking a feminine leg outside the covers so that the officers, seeing they were not sailors, would allow them to sleep in. A good captain made sure his men had lemon juice against scurvy, as well as meat, alcohol and hard bread, vegetables and fruit when available.

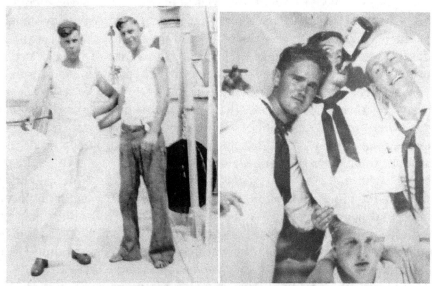

For the pleasure of the eyes - 5

THE AGE OF PIRATES

When you seek information concerning privateers' homosexuality you come across, exclusively, B.R. Burg's *Sodomy and the Pirate Tradition*, 1983. There, the case for homosexuality is conjectural only. But first, the vocabulary: The English "pirate" is derived from the Latin term *pirata* and that from Greek πειρατής (*peiratēs*), "brigand", Wikipedia informs us. Buccaneer, says Wikipedia, derives from the Caribbean Arawak word buccan, a wooden frame for smoking meat, usually manatee. From this the French derived the word *boucane* and hence the name *boucanier* for French hunters who used such frames to smoke meat over pits on Hispaniola (now Haiti and the Dominican Republic). English colonists anglicized the word *boucanier* to *buccaneer*. A privateer was a private person or ship that received government permission to attack foreign vessels.

Piracy has existed since the first boats, in Greece, in Rome and during the crusades. Herein we're going to cover the golden age of piracy, mostly in the Caribbean thanks to Spanish vessels gorged with treasure from the lands discovered by the likes of Cortés and Pizarro. I intend to exploit, especially, the period ruled by the Stewarts because it was that culture, that humus, that nourished the growth of homosexuality, thanks to James I/VI's taste for boys and men, from which came a near-total *laisser-faire* and indifference to homosexual acts, a huge change from James' predecessor, Henry VIII, a rampant heterosexual who passed the laws that had homosexuals go up in smoke at the stake. (The reason this book is dedicated to James.)

The political instability of the 1600s in England, with a civil war between Charles I and his parliament that went on for years, saw bands of youngsters on the roads, those who couldn't find a place in the servant class or refused to do so, or did so but left due to the abuse of their betters. Or boys who refused the poverty of their farmer parents, or simply the children set free to fend for themselves because they came from huge families, 8 to 12 being the mean (half of which nonetheless died young), children they rarely nourished after ages 6 to 13, most who were apprenticed in a trade, the girls most often servants, boys from age 7 handed over to farmers ever in need of labor.

Those who took to the roads were boys--with the occasional girl reserved for the chiefs--who stole to survive or begged, a commonplace for the times, and who found sex among themselves, as it was either that or its solitary alternative. In reality, sex was little more complicated than boys pissing together, although along the way friendships were certainly formed. The number of vagabonds has been *estimated* at around 30,000.

The period filled by the Stewarts was a hiatus between that of Henry VIII where homosexuality was first punished by death in 1533, the naval trials of the late 1700s where both penetration and ejaculation *in situ* had to be proven in order for a man to be put to death, to the times of Byron (1800) where one could be pilloried and/or hung, according to the gravity of the offence, and the times of Oscar Wilde (late 1800s) where lives and reputations were ruined, and men rotted in prisons of unbelievable filthiness, light years away from French *de*criminalization of sodomy in 1791.

Sodomy in the navy became a hanging offense in 1627 and in 1806 there were more hangings in England for sodomy than for murders. A sailor in 1757 received 500 lashes for raping a boy and two seamen received 1,000 lashings each in 1762 for *consensual* sex. The last man was executed in 1835, after which a man received from 10 years imprisonment to life.

The reign of James VI/I was the calm before the storm. When his son Charles was beheaded (4) the Church of England was abolished and Puritanism under Cromwell did away with not only homosexuality, but also card playing, drunkenness, cockfights and brothels. Tired of Puritanism, the reestablishment of a king, in this case Charles II, brought in a period where one could again breath, as happened in the Renaissance after the Middle Ages, meaning that there was the flourishing of what had been forbidden. One could again sin, and even theater presentations were said to have been nearly pornographic in content when compared to the years of Henry VIII.

During James's reign boy wanderers knew the ropes sexually by the time they made it to ports, and adapted to sexual practices once on board. Sexuality was a natural urge, and like any other it demanded release. The release was public because outside of the officers' cabins there was absolutely no free space. But the poor had been brought up in such conditions, where parents and children shared the same room and sex held no mysteries. The very poor, like the family of the explorer Stanley, were put in workshops as Stanley had been, several to a bed, where every form of sexual perversion known to man took place (5).

In the Royal Navy many men were shanghaied, a disgusting way of filling quotas of needed labor and cannon fodder. The treatment aboard was brutal and the officers often sadists or even psychopaths. Men were paid to impress others, perhaps getting them drunk, and fishermen were especially prized as they knew the sea already, but vagabonds or common farm boys also awoke in the holds of royal man-of-war ships. Yet in winter these men were no longer needed, and found themselves, at times thousands in certain ports, unemployed and a real danger to the populace. A part of these men found their way to pirate ships, as did men who had turned to crime and found piracy an asylum from the law.

As Spain had taken possession of the Dutch Netherlands, the Dutch ships were especially motivated to board Spanish vessels, stealing and killing all aboard. French Protestants from La Rochelle plundered Catholic Spain's treasure boats. Two Spanish possessions in the Caribbean, Hispaniola and Tortuga, were notably favored targets, where Spanish galleons lay in anchorage. On Tortuga a traitor trading post was founded that sold everything from meat to ammunitions to Spain's enemies. Spain finally massacred the inhabitants in 1635, but those who escaped went to Hispaniola where it was business as usual, most of which were in turn massacred in 1640. In the meantime, animals liberated on both islands prospered, providing huge food supplies for pirates anchoring the night in isolated bays. The men not massacred often became pirates, transforming their skills in riflemanship into wealth when they overran the gunnels of the Spanish vessels sent out to destroy them, the Spanish murderers of their families and friends. The flow of blood was constant, and Spain would be bled white, going from the richest nation in Europe to bankruptcy. Because the French were Catholics and the Dutch and English Protestants, these last two had mixed crews from both countries, while France sailed and plundered for itself. The English raided from its safe havens on the islands of Barbados, St. Christopher, Nevis, Antigua and Montserrat. All five islands were eventually farmed thanks to fertile volcanic soil, and in the course of time tobacco would become the primary cash crop. Because conditions were so rough and the voyages to the islands difficult and highly dangerous, nearly a hundred percent of the population was male, meaning that those who turned to piracy were already broken in to same-sex sexual relief. Burg brings us the testimony of one island planter who claimed that when women were available they were expensive and their flesh "clammy", whereas men were free and the relationships between them were "frank and natural" ... "and to express their affections yet higher, they had particular names as Neighbor, Friend and Brother." Between them there was "nothing wanting".

Cromwell and then Charles II sent the overflow of English convicts to islands like Jamaica, at least three men to each woman, the guarantee of a homosexual ambiance, one that continued when the men escaped and found work on the only ships that would have them, buccaneer vessels. At the same time labor was so short on the islands and ships circulating in the Caribbean that kidnappers made fortunes through what was literally called man stealing in England itself, which often included parents paid to give up their children who would find themselves as servants on some English island. Kidnapping in Bristol was such a plague that the city fathers sent delegations to complain to Cromwell. Many men voluntarily left England during the civil wars between Charles I and his parliament, hoping to improve their economic situation or even make a fortune through piracy. There is something innate to man that pushes him to believe in get-rich-quick schemes, as it does for his need for religion. To pay for the passage to Caribbean islands many men sold themselves into slavery for a numbers of years. But soon blacks took over the role of whites, as sugar production largely replaced tobacco. In Jamaica, Port Royal (part of today's Kingston) rose to fame as the Caribbean capital of debauch, where girls were obtainable, one tavern owned by a certain John Starr who employed 21 white women and 2 blacks.

Piracy was so profitable that buccaneers were solicited by even the governor of Jamaica, Thomas Modyford, and at one time 22 pirate ships were using Port Royal, each with a crew of around 60, and Burg relates that between 1688 and 1690, 280 ships stopped there. Yet the havoc produced by the lusty sailors obliged Jamaica to eventually forbid them in order to attract steady trade with peace-loving French, Spanish and Dutch. In 1678 the first anti-piracy law was adopted.

Piracy moved north, to the Bahamas and Bermuda, sites that became known for debauch, where men drank and sexually abused their neighbor's wives and even their own sisters when in the mood. This paradise came to an end in 1703 when the islanders were attacked by the Spanish and French who killed every male that came to hand and imprisoned every female, leaving the islands deserted, a Sodom and Gomorrah-size retribution.

Interestingly, black slavery only worked when there was an equal number of men and women slaves, as black men refused labor without female consolation, a complaint that didn't exist between white males.

Homosexuality was situational. The right place at the right time, meaning the Caribbean and its warm conducive climate, taverns with alcohol, the immense exhilaration caused by the capture of a ship with its wealth, sexual stimulation said to follow bloodshed, even males stripping down to careen beached ships, as well as full stomachs around campfires and the veil of dunes that provided protective privacy to couples that formed, all of which was encouraged by the moans of their companions in the midst of action, moans familiar since childhood when a family shared a single room, or on marches when boys were vagabonds.

Various sources underline the lack of importance of women sexually. One claims that the buccaneer Stede Bonnet killed all the men on a captured vessel and merely threw the only woman overboard with the ship refuse. Another that Henry Morgan captured a number of women in Porto Bello and had them locked in a church where they were fed and left untouched.

Men taken as crew members were dispersed among the other sailors, while boys were taken in hand by specific adults, usually officers. The boys, captives or shanghaied or volunteers, found nothing different, sexually, from what they had known as wanderers. The officers often took elaborate care of the youths, even giving them a share of their booty. The boys were especially prized as they were easily dominated, sexually uncritical, and less demanding than were men. Burg tells us of Captain Charles Swan who captured a lad and took him aboard despite the tears of his parents, promising them to make ''much of the boy'', which he did by assuring his education.

Even when charges were brought against an officer, they were rare because the word of a cabin-boy-former-vagabond meant nothing. And, anyway, the lad could simply be thrown overboard if need be. But when there were complaints, the specifics were deleted. Burg gives the example of a Spanish cabin boy who played along with the captain of his ship, Bartholomew Sharp, certainly in order to save his life. But once back in London the boy, Calderon, age 16, went to his embassy and complained. We know neither the charges nor the result but it seemed clear that, at the very least, the captain had been, as Burg writes, ''infatuated'' with the lad. Sharp had been an extremely capable seaman who had nonetheless been deposed in a mutiny due to setbacks in the handling of storms that he was held responsible for. He was later taken back when his replacement was killed. He is credited as the first Englishman to travel eastwards around Cape Horn, and in 1684 a book about his adventures was published. He was later jailed for debt, where he died.

On the island of Hispaniola a special structure called *matelotage* developed, *matelot* from the French word for sailor. Similar to the Australian "mate", the two men involved were sealed in a kind of informal marriage. They shared all and supposedly if one wed the other had equal rights to the woman. One *matelot* sent on ahead to inform his friend's wife that he was coming, found her in bed with another. The friend was informed and put both his wife and her lover to death.

In another incident of *matelotage* the captain of a ship was insulted by a sailor whom the captain ran through with his sword to silence him. The sailor's friend, his *matelot*, went to the captain and berated him for the death of his friend. The captain ran him through too, but didn't kill him. Later the sailor was whipped for insulting the captain. But he in turn had another friend who agreed to take half of the lashes.

The final example of *matelotage* was the story of George Rounsivil, a buccaneer who set out to strike it rich but whose ship was wrecked off Green Key Island. He found himself in a lifeboat that was hailed by his *matelot* from the stern of the sinking ship, begging him to come back for him. Rounsivil pleaded with his mates to return to the ship for his friend. When they refused--afraid the extra weight would sink them all--Rounsivil jumped overboard and returned to go down with his mate.

What took place aboard, sexually, was basically mutual masturbation, intercrural sex (between the legs) and anal intercourse. Fellatio was far less referred to during trials, on sea or on land, likely due to extremely poor hygiene. Fellatio seems to have been part of upper-class sex, certainly due to more frequent baths or perfume, although bath-taking then was in no way comparable to our own nearly fetish need to smell good.

During the American Civil War there were often long hours of doing nothing, and so one passed the time with tobacco and drinking and occasional mutual satisfaction, usually shared masturbation, mostly on ships but also on land. Even when one paid for the favors of, say, a young drummer boy, the cost was a quarter, compared to $3 for a woman. One man on a ship said that during his entire career he never met a single man who hadn't had sex afloat.

As I made clear at the outset, detailed information on pirate homosexuality is nonexistent. Illiteracy and the need to keep one's sexual practices private were partial causes. Also, because everyone--or nearly--was doing it, it was in no one's interest to bring it into the limelight. Boys knew what awaited them before boarding ships, and many may have welcomed it as a way of comradeship, of avoiding syphilis, and for release that didn't cost a penny. There was certainly abuse but as we see elsewhere in this book, because the penalty was death, the jurors had to be certain that both penetration and emission of semen took place, not easy to prove. If a cabin boy did complain, well, accidents so easily happened, as said. Foreign lads could appeal to their embassies but who wanted to cause an international scandal over something as disgusting as one man invading another's ass with his dick? But like the Oscar Wilde scandal (caused by a man who really did think he was too powerful and famous to be put in his place by mere jurors, ignoramuses in comparison to himself), some fathers did bring the cases before the courts, simply because they were not in agreement that their sons be used like disposable Kleenex.

For the pleasure of the eyes - 6

CAPTAIN ROBERT JONES'S
TRIAL 1772

I'm not going to belabor the contacts between ship officers, cabin boys and young crewmembers because much of what took place was certainly abuse of power on the part of the captains, repugnant in every aspect. Which doesn't mean that youths didn't have sincerely affectionate relations with men, captains included, or use them for their own personal advancement. The cases that follow clearly show what comprised a crime during this period.

Robert Jones was such a captain and was responsible for popularizing skating in England, in part thanks to his published book on the subject. Written for men as women didn't skate at the time, Jones's book described figure skating and figure eights, literally inventing a field that until then had been known only for speed skating. He was also known as an expert in fireworks, popularizing their usage throughout the kingdom. He was a gay blade, openly frequenting known homosexuals, although his reputation as a womanizer put him above all suspicion of harboring homosexual tendencies. In fact, he was on the verge of marrying a woman of wealth. Jones had been signaled out at the time for his disguise as Punch during one of Teresa Cornelys' famous masquerades, the entry to which, at her Carlisle House mansion, was prized by the nobility.

The story of Teresa Cornelys began when her actress mother put her on the road to seduction, teaching her how to hold off the rich and powerful until she could extract maximum value in exchange for her charms. At times she did so for pleasure, as with Casanova, to whom she bore a child, and gave up another of her children in his care, a boy Giuseppe, when she was imprisoned for debt. She adopted the name of one of her lovers, Cornelys, and took on a pimp, a cellist who worked at the theater where she made her début as an actress, a man who later claimed to be a preacher and took her to London where they opened a whorehouse under the guise of a chic salon, at a rented manor, Carlisle House, assiduously frequented by Robert Jones. Besides herself and her girls, she offered card games, dancing and masquerades--Thackeray's book *Barry Lyndon* took place there. Casanova returned later, writing that she had 32 servants and three secretaries. The rooms of her manor were so crowded that she had to outlaw hooped skirts, which took up space, and so numerous were the carriages that dropped off clients that she initiated the world's first one-way traffic system. But the wealth of the furnishings and the cost of publicity were such that she spent more money than she brought in, and eventually had to close down and auction off her belongings. She was jailed for dept, escaped, tried her hand at other sources of income, like breakfasts destined for the nobility. Her children, boys and girls, raised as aristocrats, had at least been well educated, allowing them to fend for themselves. She died in prison at age 74.

Because a man's life was at stake sodomy had to be proved beyond doubt, making two concordant conditions imperative: The anus had to be proved to have been penetrated and sperm deposited therein, a seemingly impossible task until one reads the transcript of the trial of Robert Jones, in which one admires the prosecutor's thorough attempts to arrive at the truth; his in-depth questioning; and his success in bringing facts to light. The handling of the boy witness was exemplary, for the avuncular nature of the questioner visibly put the lad at ease, enough to detail acts made sordid due to the lad's extreme youth.

Punch

The boy had been 12 at the time, but because he was but a month from his 13th birthday, it is that age which is most often referred to. Had the acts taken place but a year later the consequences would have been greatly different, as the boy would have been 14, the age of consent in England (the act of *sodomy* remaining, nonetheless, punishable by hanging). Because a man's life was in play the interrogation had to be extremely precise and the boy's character beyond reproach. And indeed, the boy rose well above his contemporaries in that he was deemed by all who knew him as serious, trustworthy, scrupulously honest in speech, acts and testimony, and such was the lad's impact on the jury.

Puberty came later at that time than today, and the boy seemed to have been sexually indifferent to what he went through, himself incapable of being aroused or achieving orgasm. Had there been masturbation alone, Jones would have faced a simple misdemeanor.

The bare facts of the matter are these: The boy's uncle had a shop that did, among other things, shoe repairs. Captain Jones was a valued customer and had had ample opportunity of observing the lad. During one visit he suggested that the boy come to his residence in search of a pair of shoes in need of a new buckle. Because Jones's manner--open, warm and amusing-- was appreciated by all, because he was important to his father's affair, and due to the possibility that he could earn a coin or two, the boy was happy to consent.

Immediately on entering Jones's apartments Jones locked the door and proceeded to fondle the boy through his trousers, before lowering the boys pants and his own, preparatory to penetration, after which he apparently had a second orgasm by masturbating on the floor. The boy was requested to return the next morning where the man masturbated himself while fondling the boy, the whole scandal ending in a third visit where the same masturbatory act was repeated. The boy was paid all three times, trifling amounts in today's terms but back then a house could be rented for a shilling.

At home the lad fell ill and was bedded with pain between his thighs. Humiliated for what he had done for a few coppers, he kept the provenance of his suffering--the exact area and what had taken place--to himself.

Jones returned to the shop and requested that the boy deliver a pair of shoes he had ordered. When he left, the boy admitted to a friend of his uncle's that he didn't wish to go. The friend pursued the matter when the boy's uncle had left the shop on an errand, and the boy, yearning to get it off his chest, admitted all, the genesis of the trial and the following transcript. The boy's name is Hay:

Q. How old are you?

Hay. I shall be thirteen next January.

Q. Are you to tell the truth?

Hay. Yes.

Q. What do you know against the prisoner?

Hay. I was walking up St. Martin's Lane, I believe on Tuesday.

Q. Did you go to school?

Hay. Yes, I did. I live with my uncle a jeweler in Parliament Street. I met Captain Jones the prisoner, in St. Martin's Lane. He told me he had a buckle to mend.

Q. How long is that ago?

Hay. I believe about a month ago. He took me up stairs into his lodgings, in St. Martin's Court. He took me into his dining room, and he locked the door.

Q. Had you ever been in company with him before?

Hay. No. He always used to look at me, and give me halfpence when he met me. He pulled down my breeches and then his own.

Q. Were not you frightened at this?

Hay. Yes, I was a little. He set me in an elbow chair; he set me down and kissed me a little; then he made me lay down with my face on the chair, and so he came behind me; he put his cock into my hole.

Q. Did you submit to it quietly, or make any resistance?

Hay. I submitted to it quietly.

Q. How long might he keep it in your hole?

Hay. About five minutes I believe.

Q. Was he quite in?

Hay. A little.

Q. Was he in at all?

Hay. Yes.

Q. Did you find anything come from him?

Hay. Some wet stuff that was white; I wiped it off.

Q. Can you describe to the jury how far it was in your body?

Hay. No.

Q. What did you wipe the wet off with?

Hay. My shirt.

Q. You are sure it was in you?

Hay. Yes.

Q. What did he do after this?

Hay. He spouted some on the ground.

Q. Did he spout some into your hole?

Hay. Yes.

Q. What did he do after this?

Hay. He set me down in the elbow chair, kissed me a little, and gave me some halfpence and told me not to tell anybody.

Q. How long did you stay?

Hay. About half an hour.

Q. Did he attempt to do anything more to you?

Hay. No, not then.

Q. How came you not to cry out?

Hay. I was ashamed.

Q. Had ever anybody served you in this manner before?

Hay. No.

Q. Did you tell your uncle, or anybody, when you came home?

Hay. No.

Q. How soon did you go again?

Hay. He desired me to come next day; I went; he unbuttoned my breeches again, and then his own.

Q. What time did you go next day?

Hay. About eleven o'clock. He made me rub his cock up and down till some white stuff came again.

Q. At the time he put his cock into your hole, it was stiff and hard, was it?

Hay. Yes.

Q. Did he attempt anything behind then?

Hay. No.

Q. How long did you stay with him then?

Hay. About ten minutes.

Q. You quietly submitted to all that?

Hay. Yes. He gave me the buckle and some halfpence then, and desired me to come again next day; I went next day about eleven o'clock. He unbuttoned his breeches again, and mine too. He did the same again that time as he did the last day.

Q. What happened next?

Hay. I was taken very ill after this. I was ill a week. I had a pain in my thighs and legs that I could not stand. About a fortnight ago, after I was well, he came to the shop one day, and looked on the show glasses. He bespoke a shirt buckle of my uncle. It was to be sent home to him. My uncle ordered me to go with the buckle. I told him he had better go, and perhaps he might get the captain's business.

Q. When you went so willingly two days together after the first offence was committed, how came you to make the objection to go now?

Hay. I was afraid he would serve me the same thing again.

Q. How came you to object to go now and not before?

Hay. He told me not to tell of it, and I was ashamed. The reason was because I was so ill.

Q. Did you think you had been doing a wrong thing?

Hay. Yes. As soon as he left the shop I told Mr. Rapley of it. He is a jeweler.

Q. What time was it the captain came to look at the show glass?

Hay. About twelve o'clock.

Q. How came you to tell Mr. Rapley, and not tell your uncle?

Hay. I was ashamed to tell my uncle.

Q. Did you go there before dinner?

Hay. Yes.

Q. Did you tell your uncle the whole story, how he had served you these three times?

Hay. I told him what he had done to me the first time, but not the last times.

Q. How came you to tell it now, when you kept it a secret so long.

Hay. I thought I would tell of it all the while, but I was ashamed.

Q. Did you think you had been doing a wrong thing with him.

Hay. Yes.

Q. Then how came you to go of your own accord the second and third times?

Hay. I thought my uncle might get business by it.

Q. Did anything more happen than what you have told us now?

Hay. No.

The newspapers related that it took the jury 5 minutes to reach a decision, death by hanging, a verdict later rescinded in exchange for Jones's exile from England, for which he was allowed two weeks. The clemency granted by the king was due to a petition by a large number of notables who vouched for Jones's character, with the exception of this brief error in judgment. In reality, Jones--like a huge percentage of the English who had undergone boyhood boarding-school adventures--was bisexual, and it was most probable that usually Jones found contentment with adolescents, not pre-pubic children like Hay.

One paper claimed he went to Florence for a time, not the worst of exiles, and then to Lyons where, said another paper, he lived with his footboy (male domestic worker). He was reported as going to Turkey where he served assorted Beys, but during a conflict that arose between several pretenders to the throne, he championed the wrong side and had his head separated from his body.

For the pleasure of the eyes – 7

WILLIAM BERRY'S
TRIAL 1807

The valiant military history of the 16-gun sloop the *Hazard*, commissioned in 1794, would take pages to cover. Its crew was decorated numerous times for its action during the French Revolution and the Napoleonic Wars. It captured numerous privateers, most of which outgunned the *Hazard* and had more men aboard, in one case 150 in comparison to the sloop's 106, as well as boarding a score of enemy ships, burning others, and landing men to capture islands and invade towns.

A Sloop

The incident that interests us took place in 1807 when the first lieutenant William Berry, 22, was hung for a homosexual attack on a cabin boy, Thomas Gibbs. Berry was hung but the hanging was so botched that 32 pounds of shot had to be attached to his feet, Berry taking an additional 15 minutes to strangle to death. With the exception of Captain Henry Allen of the *Rattler* (about whom details are lacking), this was the only officer hung for sodomy during the wars against Napoleon.

The prime witness to Berry's act of sodomy had been, bizarrely, a woman who had been a passenger on the ship, and whose curiosity concerning male anatomy may have been the cause of her spying on Berry, that all described as extremely handsome and well-made, through the keyhole of his door.

For the pleasure of the eyes - 8

HERMAN MELVILLE
1819 – 1891

Herman Melville was a sailor at age 17 in 1837, a year in which one simply did not publish books that were homosexually oriented. Melville's greatest love seems to have been Captain Jack Chase, to whom he dedicated *Billy Budd.*

Dedicated
To
JACK CHASE
Englishman
Wherever that great heart may now be
Here on Earth or harbored in Paradise
Captain of the Maintopin the year 1843in the U.S. Frigate*United States*

Male-male sex was prevalent onboard ships as well as in taverns, bars, shipyards and the parks surrounding docking areas. For the homoerotic symbolism of *Moby Dick* I'm relying on the interpretations of others, many other, because I missed them all when I read the book as a young man, as I did Cellini's wondrous love for boys, so clearly stated in his autobiography that was among the books generously offered by the Peace Corps to new volunteers, but I was of the pre-Internet generation, not only unable to recognize homosexuality in others, and in Melville's books, but largely ignorant of my own.

At any rate, in *Moby Dick* Ishmael, in bed, watches the cannibal Queequeg, a harpooner, who undresses before him, showing his "bald purplish head", jumping into bed with his "tomahawk", the whole causing Ishmael to "shriek out" and "kick about", awaking the next morning "ambiguously intertwined" and, like Scarlett O'Hara after her first night with Rhett Butler, thinking I "never slept better in my life." "Queequeg's arm thrown over me in the most loving and affectionate manner," "you had almost thought I have been his wife." Referring also to "his bridegroom clasp" (filling us in on who had been the top and who the bottom), "hugging a fellow male in that matrimonial sort of style." "Thus, then, in our hearts' honeymoon, lay I and Queequeg--a cozy, loving pair."

In his book *Pierre* we find this: "In their boyhood and earlier adolescence, Pierre and Glen had cherished a much more than cousinly attachment. At the age of ten, they had furnished an example of the truth, that the friendship of fine-hearted, generous boys, nurtured amid the romance-engendering comforts and elegancies of life, sometimes transcends the bounds of mere boyishness, and revels for a while in the empyrean of a love which only comes short by one degree, of the sweetest sentiment entertained between the sexes. Nor is this boy-love without the occasional fillips and spicinesses, which at times, by an apparent abatement, enhance the permanent delights of those more advanced lovers who love beneath the cestus of Venus." (Even now, years after the Peace Corps, it's still hard to figure out what the hell he's referring to.) At that same age my own cousin and I were sporting and limitlessly comparing erections, having a hell of a good time, years before either one of us knew what else they could be used for. But then came puberty and my cousin's interest in girls, and my own sex life dried up until that memorable day in the Salle des Vases greque in the Louvre, so many wasted years later (1).

Melville served on the *USS United States* from 1843 to 1844, from which experience came his novel *White-Jacket* that condemned flogging and, thanks to Melville's fame, was read by congressmen who abolished flogging for all time. (The battle in the senate to end flogging was led by John Hale, whose daughter was the fiancée of John Wilkes Booth.) Melville called ships "wooden-walled Gomorrahs of the deep". He called marriage "a form of suicide" although he did enter into an unhappy union.

Melville's father, of French origin, provided the boy with an excellent schooling and digs with servants until his death from pneumonia when the boy was 13, obliging him to enter his uncle's bank at age 14. Thanks to inheritances he was able to continue his schooling later on, but throughout his entire adolescence he was an avid reader, books which apparently inspired his later writing, as he took notes of his favorite passages and descriptions. He prized public speaking and debates, and two early works of his, on politics, made it into the papers, when he was 19. Inspired by the book *Two Years Before the Mast* he signed on as a "green hand" on the whaler Acushnet for 1/175th of the profits, remuneration then in practice, used even on pirate ships. He deserted in the Marquises Islands and spent time island hopping until enlisting on the *USS United States*, his experiences written up in his books *Typee, Omoo* and *White-Jacket*.

Because his books didn't sell well, and some reviews were humiliating, he got work as a customs inspector for the city of N.Y. He had confided to his intimate friend Hawthorne that he contemplated suicide, a choice his son Malcolm took at age 18, at the end of a shotgun. His second son Stanwix died at age 36 of illness. Melville himself died at age 72 in 1891. Around 1930 there began a Melville revival, the epicenter of which was Yale University.

For the pleasure of the eyes – 9

THE BLOOMSBURY SET

To understand the Bloomsbury Set one must understand the French expression *panier de crabes*, a basket of crabs, crawling over and through each other, fucking, yes, but also biting, their claws fully deployed.

A perfect example of this was Duncan Grant's relationship with Vanessa Bell. Duncan, a painter and a homosexual who had had exclusively homosexual encounters in boarding schools since puberty, decided to live with Vanessa who was nonetheless married but whose husband was off elsewhere with mistresses. Vanessa (the sister of Virginia Wolfe) badly wanted a child from the supremely handsome Duncan who agreed to move in with her for the time needed to get her pregnant, and immediately afterwards sexual relations ceased between the two while awaiting the birth of their little girl, Angelica, who was given Bell's name, Bell who pretended to be her father.

Duncan Grant

Duncan stayed on with Vanessa, which in no way inhibited his taking numerous lovers, for 40 years, until her death. One of his lovers was David Garnett who later married Angelica. Garnett was thusly fucking the father *and* the father's daughter! (although, perhaps, not at the same time).

David Garnett by Duncan.

Maynard Keynes said Duncan Grant had been the love of his life. From his youth Duncan had been one of Lytton Strachey's lovers, Strachey who was also his cousin. He was also the lover of Arthur Hobhouse. Hobhouse entered Eton at age 11 and then Balliol College, Oxford, seven years later. He had his own law practice, was on the board of a charity commission, worked as a law member for the council of the Governor-General of India, and was on the Judicial Committee of the Privy Council when he returned from India to London. He received a peerage as Baron Hobhouse, married and died without children.

Duncan Grant with Keynes and picture of Hobhouse, age 35.

Duncan was kept during his later life by Paul Roche and it was on Roche's estate that he died.

Roche by Duncan Grant.

Duncan was born in 1885, just six months before the passing of the Criminal Law Act that criminalized male homosexual acts in England, regardless of consent, an act used to convict Oscar Wilde in 1895. It was also dubbed the blackmailer's act because it was profitably used by hundreds of blackmailers afterwards (many of whom committed suicide when outed). The fear of discovery was such that even later writers on Greek love, such as A.L. Rowse and Kenneth Dover, claimed to have been happily married, which, conceivably, could have been true.

Paul Roche by Duncan.

Duncan went to prep schools in Rugby and London before entering the Westminster School of Art at age 17.

Hyllus by Duncan.

What seems incredible, at least to me, is that men like Grant were having sex with some of the homeliest men living then. Of course I'll be accused of being shallow, but a man does have to get hard to have good sex, and how can one do so in the presence of men like Keynes and Garnett?

Paul Roche and perhaps an example of boarding-school fun,
by Duncan Grant.

Paintings by Duncan are innumerable, and I've included a number here for the pleasure of the senses.

Leigh Farnell, one of Duncan's very first boarding-school friends,
with whom he remained close all his life.

Duncan was unanimously described as being a good person and those who cared for him at the end of his life found him ''impishly benign'', with great personal charm. He admired the philosopher G. E. Moore and told the boys who gave access to his old hands that he owed all of his moral philosophy to Moore, ''which possibly does not amount to much,'' probably among the truest words he ever spoke!

Duncan Grant of himself.

Another of his daughter's lovers, who had also been *his* lover, was George Bergen:

George Bergen

David Garnett, Grant's lover and Angelica's husband, was called Bunny since his childhood due to a rabbit cloak given to him then. When he married Angelica her parents were said to have been scandalized (although *which* parents, Vanessa and Bell or Vanessa and Grant, is not known). Garnett was an author, founded the Nonesuch Press and ran a bookshop. From a first wife he had had two sons and with Angelica four daughters before they separated. He died in France in 1981 at age 89.

Paul Roche was a novelist, poet and Greek and Latin translator, and was associated with the Bloomsbury Set. He was an ordained priest and married twice, fathering five children. Although Roche's last wife was against his taking in his lover, Duncan was imposed on the household but was said to have cooled things down out of respect for Roche's wife although, of course, men always succeed in getting what they want, in one secret place or another, so the cooling was most probably due to a greater desire to have sex with others than themselves.

Grant and David Garnett.

Duncan Grant died in 1978 at age 93 and Roche at age 91 in 2007. They had been together 32 years.

Paul Roche

Roche and Duncan's love had been the closest, the deepest, the truest of friendships, and Roche closes the chapter on their lives in this way: ''I could see that he was in a very bad way, breathing heavily.... Dr Cooper said to me, 'I can't save him this time, he's too far gone, and it's much better to let him go'. So I agreed to that. Duncan lay on the bed.... I came up to him the night before he died... This is what I think I said, or the gist of it.... 'Duncan, you have nothing to worry about, whatever you have done in life that you are sorry for, God loves you, whatever you've done, He loves you. You don't have to worry about anything. You're in His hands, and so you can sleep peacefully and everything is ok.... Don't think that God is angry with anything.... He's not, He loves you.' Duncan was incapable of speaking ... so I quietly left the room.... When I came back in the morning ... I realised Duncan was dead. That was an enormous shock to me.... I went to Firle to be at the funeral, but I suddenly found that I couldn't stand, every time I stood up I simply collapsed onto the floor.''

Duncan Grant's *The Bathers*.

One of the characteristics of the Bloomsbury Set, besides the fact that most lived so long, was that many ended up spending the last of their lives with women, as did Lytton Strachey and Maynard Keynes.

The Set was against what Roger Fry (who had been Vanessa Bell's lover) called Post-Impressionists, although Fry, an artist and art critic, defended it. Loved by many Bloomsbury members, male and female, he seems to have been heterosexual. His list of Post-Impressionists includes Cézanne, Gauguin, van Gogh and Seurat, to which he later added Rousseau and Toulouse-Lautrec. Many of the Set thought the Post-Impressionists were trivial in their art, reducing objects to basic shapes, while Seurat even painted tiny dots that some called Scientific-Impressionism. Van Gogh used lavish brush strokes to convey his feelings and state of mind, and Cézanne tried to bring purity in his art by reducing objects to basic shapes.

Roger Fry

Lytton Strachey, one of the founders of the Bloomsbury Set, seduced them all, and although he was presentable when very young, I have no idea how he did it later on, especially when he grew the beard he was so proud of, but that most others found ridiculous.

One of 13 children, Lytton is the 3rd from the left.

Perhaps Roy Campbell, a poet and satirist, had him in mind when he said that the Set was a group of ''sexless folk whose sexes intersect.'' Some, happily, were far from being sexless. Duncan Grant was gorgeous, and when Strachey had intercourse with him he said that he felt joy because Grant was so moved and that what he loved ''more than the consummation of my own poor pleasure ... was that for the first time I loved his soul,'' a need by the Set to introduce Plato somewhere in their sexual musical chairs. As a lad Strachey justified sex by saying that ''I may be sinning, but I am doing it in the company of Greece'' in reference to Socrates and other texts on Hellenic love. Strachey goes on and on about the ideal love, the meeting of the minds, but Roger Senhouse, a student of Eton and Oxford University and owner of the publishing house that published Colette, Orwell and Günter Grass, said his relationship with Strachey had been sadomasochistic. In the same way that Plato went on about Platonic love, stating that ''evil is the vulgar lover who loves the body rather than the soul,'' Plato and Socrates had nonetheless special permission to attend the athletic preparation of boys, where adults were banned by law, to enjoy the beauty of youthful dicks with their first pubic down, and hairless asses.

Strachey: He was proud of the reddish hue of his beard.

Strachey wrote his book *Ermyntrude and Esmeralda* in 1913, published in 1969, long after his death, in which two innocent girls titter about the ''absurd little things that men have in statues between their legs.'' When the girls asked a priest what love is, he replies "the sanctification of something", unless the object is a member of the same sex. A father banishes his son for having sex with his tutor, but the son claims that he was only doing what the Athenians did and, anyway, his father "had done the same when he was a boy in school but had forgotten about it."

Strachey's school was Trinity College, Cambridge, where he had sexual relations with Clive Bell who married Vanessa who would have sexual relations with Duncan Grant who would have sexual relations with Strachey and David Garnett, Garnett who would have sexual relations with Duncan Grant and, later, Grant's daughter Angelica, as reported.

Strachey was a member of the Apostles and the founder of the Bloomsbury Set, along with many of the aforementioned boys, in addition to Vanessa's sister who would become, through marriage, Virginia Woolf. Bloomsbury was a location in central London encompassing Gordon and Fitzroy Squares. The aim of Bloomsbury was "to get a maximum of pleasure out of their personal relations. If this meant triangles or more complicated geographical figures, well then, one accepted that too."

The Apostles was a discussion group that met weekly over coffee and "whales" (sardines on toast) to discuss a topic later thrown open to discussion. Former members were Angels, new members Embryos. The bond between them all was life-long. The spies Burgess, MacLean and Philby were members.

Strachey's hallmark was biography, combining psychology with sympathy for the subject, irreverence and wit. He wrote *Queen Victoria, Eminent Victorians* and *Elizabeth and Essex.* An example of his wit: He described Florence Nightingale as employing soldiers' wives to clean her laundry. When Strachey, a pacifist, was asked what he would do if a Hun tried to rape his sister, he answered: "I would insert my body between them." While others seduced by making girls laugh, he did so through spellbinding eloquence (maintained his admirers).

In another of those strange Bloomsbury multi-cornered sexual relationships, Strachey lived with Dora Carrington who adored him and she married *his* lover Ralph Partridge, not for love, but to bring Strachey closer to her. At the same time he was seeing other men, one of whom was Roger Senhouse, with whom he had his sadomasochistic arrangement, one that went so far as to include mock crucifixions. Strachey paid for the marriage between Carrington and Partridge and, naturally, accompanied them on their honeymoon to Venice. Carrington had a boy's haircut and appreciated girls, while her new husband was said to have genuinely loved her. Strachey bought the newly weds a house. Partridge left her for another woman and she became pregnant by another man who asked her to leave Strachey. She chose instead to abort. Around this time Aldous Huxley fell in love with her, "Her short hair, clipped like a page's.... She had large blue china eyes ... of puzzled earnestness."

Carrington and Strachey, Huxley and Senhouse.

The plot thickens: Ralph Partridge had left both Carrington and Strachey for another woman, Frances Marshall, who took up with Ralph because she knew he was Strachey's lover, and as she loved Strachey she thought her proximity with Ralph would bring her closer to Strachey.

Strachey and Partridge.

When Strachey died in 1932 at age 51 from stomach cancer, Carrington committed suicide.

Strachey must have been a force of nature because he was a character in nearly all the books his friends wrote before and after his death.

The plot doesn't end here: The painter Mark Gertler adored Carrington to the point of obsession. Incapable of understanding why she preferred a homosexual to him, he bought a revolver and threatened to kill himself when she married Strachey's lover Ralph Partridge. Gertler did finally commit suicide in 1939 at age 48. Today his paintings are worth millions.

Mark Gertler, said to have been a beauty.

In her diary Virginia Woolf wrote that she was glad to be alive and couldn't imagine why Carrington had killed herself. Ten years later, in 1941, Virginia did the same, by drowning.

E.M. Forester was above all a humanist, acknowledged as such when named President of Cambridge Humanists in 1959 and a member of the British Humanist Association from 1963 until his death in 1970 at age 81. A great aunt left him £800,000 in today's money, which freed him from any form of servitude. He was an on-the-fringe member of Bloomsbury, and a Kings College, Cambridge, student. His name is associated with several men, among them Isherwood and Benjamin Britten.

His travels took him throughout Europe, especially Italy, which inspired two books, *Where Angels Fear to Tread* and *A Room with a View*. He was secretary to a maharaja and several visits to India inspired his most read book, *A Passage to India*.

Among what is called his "loving relationships" was a very long one with a married policeman.

He was nominated for the Nobel Prize 13 times!

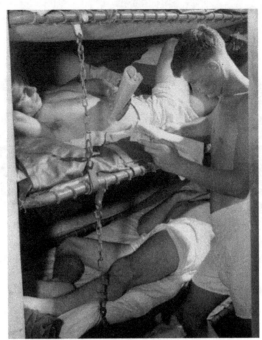

For the pleasure of the eyes - 10

THE NEWPORT SCANDAL OF 1919

The Newport Scandal could have taken place in any port or other facility catering to military personnel throughout America. It came to light in such a strange way that its catalyst is, today, of at least equal interest to the events themselves. The instigator was a simple Machinist's Mate who had been in the navy for fourteen years, but had been, before, a detective in Connecticut for nine years. His name was Ervin Arnold, and during his hospitalization for rheumatism he came upon a sailor who told him about the homosexual contacts taking place in several parts of the city of Newport, areas like the Army and Navy YMCA, cruising grounds known as the Cliff Walk and elsewhere.

The incredible Machinist's Mate put his equally incredible energy into getting a number of wheels in motion, so that a simple complaint to the station commander worked its was up to the Assistant Secretary of the Navy, none other than Franklin Delano Roosevelt, the future President of the United States, and although Roosevelt would be splattered when a certain amount of xxx hitting the fan, the year of the scandal was 1919 and would be entirely forgotten by the time of the presidential race of 1933.

Arnold, in his forties, was allowed to form a team of boys aged 17 to their early twenties, handsome of course, who went after the navy queers with such enthusiasm that the number of one boy's blowjobs was described as *prodigious* by some, *staggering* by others. Two boys had anal intercourse to orgasm, and most slept over with their marks, nude. Although we'll never know what went on in detail because none of the boys would ever admit to doing anything that put his masculinity in question, the information that came during the closed hearings was explicit to say the least (or so rumor has it). The boy-detectives claimed they did what heterosexual "trade" does for money, allowing themselves to be masturbated and sucked, while they actively fucked their prey. They never ever dropped to their knees, they swore, nor took it up the ass, nor, especially, ever allowed any kissing--the ultimate taboo. In fact, what happened was a carbon-copy of what took place in ancient Rome where men would do what they wanted with boys as long as they *always* had the male role, meaning they were the tops, the boys the bottoms, even if what really went on in the secret of the bedroom will forever be unknown.

What has dribbled down to us, perhaps by those attending the trials, was a comment concerning one guy whose chin was the perfect platform to rest a pair of balls, while another could draw a guy's brains out through his prick, so good was he at sucking, which is exactly the feeling one has when blown to perfection.

Actually, the boy-detectives' assignment was to glean information in three areas: 1) who was taking cocaine and selling liquor, 2) which females were prostituting themselves and 3) who was homosexually involved. As far as the boys were concerned, the first two were of no interest.

After a summer in prison seventeen sailors were court-marshaled and two were dishonorably discharged, while two others were freed.

The real scandal, which grew from this original one, was the use of underage boys to entrap the sailors, boys confided to the navy by trusting parents, boys who were visibly pleased when it came out that during the encounters they had been complemented on the size of their cocks, as well as their performing enthusiastically and tirelessly (the boys missing, apparently, the irony in both adjectives).

Of course, civilian members of the community were involved, many highly placed, and, naturally, there were priests and clergymen, whose sad attempts at sexual satisfaction I won't go into here, especially as I don't know which is more disgusting, this scum whose vocation it is to protect children, or the parents who continue to place there kids in their hands, despite all the warnings not to do so.

All those imprisoned were freed in 1920.

Today sailors returning from sea duty can be met by their boyfriends on the docks where they kiss publicly, but they may not hurry home to empty balls full of six months of pent-up want, as sailors throughout time did before them, not when they may have had more fun aboard than the discothèques and backrooms awaiting them on shore.

For the pleasure of the eyes - 11

THE BATTLESHIP POTEMKIN
1925

Potemkin was Catherine the Great's minister, a man of prodigious intelligence, capable of winning wars and founding whole cities, Catherine's lover when he was younger, a man devoted and loyal to her.

Eisenstein's 1925 film devoted to the Russian Revolution, *The Battleship Potemkin*, was, amazingly, banned in London, France, Germany and ever the United States for being a blueprint on how to foment a mutiny. An American critic noted Eisenstein's eye for male beauty and the film director Nestor Almendros wrote about the film's ''all-male cast ... shirtless in their hammocks ... [the cannons that] are raised to fire, a sort of visual ballet of multiple slow and pulsating erections.'' Ronald Bergan in his excellent article on the film notes that Eisenstein ''was slyly playing with the slowly rising guns as well as the scenes with sailors polishing pistons in a masturbatory manner. There are also the fleeting shots of two sailors obviously kissing as the cannons rise.'' In one scene a lad tears open his shirt in fury, a scene, Bergan tells us, that Eisenstein claimed interested him more than the raising of the red flag at the conclusion.

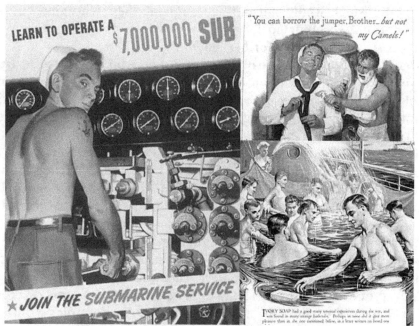

For the pleasure of the eyes - 12

SAILORS AND SEX IN PRE-WWI BERLIN

What is amazing in the history of love among males was that after the Renaissance there followed an age darker than the Middle Ages which had preceded the Renaissance. Love between males during the Renaissance could be punished by death, but in reality under Lorenzo *Il Magnifico* de' Medici one got off easily because everyone was doing it, sharing, at some point in their lives, an orgasm with another male. As girls were worth their weight in gold thanks to advantageous marriages that would enrich their husbands, they were kept locked away. Unlike a boy who could offer himself to a hundred passing hands or mouths or anuses and still claim innocence, a girl had one chance, after which the fruit was eternally spoiled.

After the Renaissance we stepped back into the dark, where lads, in the 1800s, could not comprehend their attraction to lads, those they had seen swimming in rivers and lakes, naked and so beautiful the boys dreaming of them inundated their own bellies in equally wondrous rivers and lakes. Till then, men were thought (by some) to have become homosexual because they were so insatiable sexually that they simply turned to men as an alternative to women who now bored them. Sexuality was malleable, and one could alter it at will. To keep boys on the right track laws were harsh, although thankfully the death penalty had been dropped, except, in one of life's never-ending paradoxes, in Berlin--until 1868. It was felt that men who cared for other men were in reality women trapped in a man's body, which would not only account for their searching out other men, but would account too for those who were effeminate. The woman within was seeking an outlet for her femininity.

Men who were lucky, mostly educated men who emigrated to Berlin, could find sexual satisfaction in the garrison city of 400,000 where soldiers and sailors padded their pay by selling themselves, and that for generations. The unlucky ones, the vast majority, may have felt that they and their sexuality were alone in the world, that no others shared their dreams and lust. These would live and die alone. Following the French Revolution laws against sodomy were abolished in France in 1791. Under French influence they were abolished also in Spain, Belgium, the Netherlands and Italy. Certain parts of Germany followed. In Bavaria, for example, only those who raped other men or who had sex with boys under 12 were prosecuted. But in all parts of Germany men could be imprisoned if they did something against public decency, a seemingly normal demand since having sex, for example, in the middle of a public street (homosexual or heterosexual sex), struck everyone as bad form. The law, in reality however, was diverted to cover whatever the police wanted it to cover. An example: a boy who related to another boy how he had been fucked--but well paid--in a park, was overheard by a woman who was shocked, a public act of indecency because the boys had spoken in public. The boy was found and jailed. But even this liberalism was revoked following several horrendous rapes of minors, and in 1871 laws were again reenacted in Germany against sodomy.

The population of Berlin exploded, from the 400,000 to 4 million in 1920. Berlin went from a city of open sewers to the first city ever electrified, with, in 1800, electric streetcars and lighting. It went from a city of open sewers to one of public toilets and baths, from the filthiest to the cleanest city in the world, infinitely more hygienic than London, Paris and N.Y. At the end of the 1400s in Florence the Office of the Night was formed to put an end to sodomy. The penalty was death but everyone got off with a slap on the wrist, except those who forced children to have sex. In 1885 Berlin established the Department of Homosexuals, proof of the growing number of gays. The police collected information and mug shots of homosexuals, and encouraged doctors and educators to study Berlin's unique sexual subculture, thanks to which reams of information concerning the sexuality of the times have come to us. In 1896 the name of the Department of Homosexuals was changed to Department of Homosexuals and Blackmailers. More money could be gained by pimps putting 14-year-old boys on the streets and then blackmailing the clients. In 1902 Friedrich Alfred Krupp, the Cannon King, committed suicide when blackmail led to the publication of his preference for Italian boys. For such a rich, powerful man to end his own life so young spoke volumes about being branded a homosexual, about the prevalence of blackmail and about the availability of underage lads. The department store magnate Hermann Israel killed himself on his yacht at age 40 when his companion blackmailed him. Before dying Israel turned the boy's threatening letters over to the police. The lad was sentenced to two months imprisonment. Victims of blackmail numbered in the hundreds, two of whom were well-known jurists, one who shot his blackmailer when he literally didn't have a cent left to pay him off. In 1902 a 28-year-old ophthalmologist committed suicide when his card was found in a boy's jacket and the ophthalmologist was threatened with a trial. At the time, it was established that a third of Berlin's homosexuals were being blackmailed. But as Berlin's reputation for male prostitution bloomed, johns from all over Europe flocked to the world's greatest center of boys.

Although boy whorehouses would number in the hundreds in the pre-WWI years of Christopher Isherwood, the beginnings in the very early 1900s were rudimentary, where everyone from a club owner to a tobacconist could use a backroom for financial gain, recruiting hustlers, soldiers and sailors from off the streets. Any man could have a room and rent out his boys, as pimps have since the beginning of time. And as the boys were often twelve to fifteen, their suitors could be either blackmailed or robbed while busy with their young prey. Any schoolboy or shop boy, any servant or thief, sailor or soldier, could round off monthly earnings by playing innocent or butch or changing into drag.

Rich men like Friedrich Alfred Krupp, as stated, were openly blackmailed, or writers would threaten to publish tell-all books if they didn't pay up. Some hustlers trailed likely johns and then, catching hold of them, accused them of soliciting and threatened to call the police. Robert Beachy in his wonderful *Gay Berlin* (2014) tells us that this at times ended in jail terms for the blackmailer, and the boys could be clobbered by the men they pursued, especially if, as in one case, the target was a bullish butcher, but these brave citizens were most probably the vast minority.

What happened next was pretty much inexplicable to rationalists. As clubs gained in number so did those who took advantage of johns, robbing and blackmailing them. More and more targets were out-of-town Germans (city dwellers became streetwise), many well-off merchants and industrialists. This in turn inspired more boys to go to Berlin, which in turn drew still more men seeking youths. Soon the British came, followed by Americans. Those who sought and bought sex returned home to flaunt the merits of Berlin's boys, often hung, often highly-sexed lads who, because of their growing numbers, cost less and less. The minority of men robbed and otherwise extorted turned more and more to the police who had such complete files on the boys, largely thanks to the effective Chief of Police Leopold von Meerscheidt-Hüllessem, that the lads were often apprehended and the stolen goods retrieved. This made great copy for newspapers, thanks to which more and more foreigners learned about Berlin's boys. More rent and johns flocked to the new gay oasis, in (small) part responsible for its population exploding to 4 million, including (according to one estimate) a pre-WWI total of 170 boy bordellos. More than an oasis, Berlin became an earthly heaven because every variation of sex was represented, because beer and liquor flowed, because of hugely successful floorshows, as seen in Isherwood's *Cabaret*.

That said, many German boys practiced sports that kept their bodies trim, and naked sunbathing took place around lakes, along rivers and even in public swimming pools, thanks to which the boys were beautifully tanned. Many foreign lads, especially the English, the opposite of this, hesitated to denude themselves. Yet sex at the time was so free that one of them, Stephen Spender, at first unwilling to expose his physique, soon found himself at home in Berlin, and as far as love was concerned, "all one had to do was undress". German boys tended to be masculine, they liked to exercise and they liked to show off their toned bodies. Their smiles were often ravaging, they enjoyed roughhousing, and sexually were highly experienced. Compared to the English they were animals, studs to British boarding-school lads who were used to lying on their stomachs in wait of the thrill of penetration, something many boys beg for. Of his intimate friend Pieps, Auden said, "I like sex and Pieps likes money. It's a good exchange."

Men and youths caught breaking Paragraph 175 got off with a minimal fine or a few days behind bars although blackmailers were imprisoned, one of whom got ten years. But as Beachy points out, between 1904 and 1920 only *two men* were caught in *flagrante delicto* and tried under the accursed Paragraph!

Kiosks were literally flooded with dozens of publications, and the kiosk owners didn't hesitate to have some pinned open, showing nude males. In 1930 Berlin had 280,000 tourists a year, among which were 40,000 Americans. There were believed to have been 100,000 rent-boys, all out for money to live on or pocket change, 1/3rd were believed to have been heterosexual. And they were cheap, especially soldiers and sailors going for 50 pfennig. Thomas Mann discovered Berlin at age 17. Christopher Isherwood refused to spend more than 10 marks, dinner and a few drinks for his boys (although this was outrageously overpaying), W.H. Auden, in his diary, detailed his sexual encounters, and the architect Philip Johnson claimed to have learned German through the horizontal method.

Auden, Spender and Isherwood

Isherwood and a friend.

Neither minors nor anyone badly dressed were admitted to the clubs in west Berlin, called the West End. In the East End everyone could enter. Sex was tame some high-class clubs, (although no-holds-barred was the rule in boy whorehouses). At the urinals boys flashed their wares, and at tables boys allowed johns to put their hands through their pockets, which had been cut away inside to allow seizure of the lads' dicks. Lederhosen was popular in the butch places Isherwood frequented, showing off boys' suntanned thighs. Isherwood was said to have had 500 during the time he was there, from 1929 to 1933. Today, boys can do that in a year, easily, but here we're talking about quantity. Quality is a completely different story. Scotty Bowers in his fascinating book *Full Service* relates that heterosexuals who requested his services rarely asked for more than a redhead or big tits, while homosexuals were extremely demanding. And it's true. That was the problem in Berlin. The beautiful boys were in private clubs and in private hands, wealthy hands, hands that could offer far more than Isherwood's ten marks, even if ten marks were extremely generous for what was available. The boys who went with Isherwood thought he was fabulously rich because they were fabulously lacking in the attributes that would place them in an entirely different class. That said, Isherwood wrote that there were so many postulants that he always found a handsome lad for the night.

Boys of quality in pre-WWI Berlin were in private hands,
not Auden and Isherwood's.

Then, as today, coke was ubiquitous, except that it had just been invented, by Albert Niemann, and was not only fully accepted, it was recommended by Freud to his patients. Klaus Mann preferred heroine but also took cocaine, said to circulate like cigarettes, and everyone was into other drugs, like morphine and opium. After using coke one writer said, ''I felt exhilarated, strong and capable of going on without tiredness.'' Some doctors and researchers believed that men became homosexual when using cocaine, that the drug was the cause, while most believed that coke simply lessened inhibitions, which liberated men with latent homosexuality or bisexuality to free themselves from self-imposed restraints. Cocaine helped one become more sociable and less shy.

Lederhosen provided immediate and all-inclusive access.

In Berlin Auden, Isherwood and their friend Spender spent their time in the Furbinger Strasse, the gay area with its male brothels, and where Auden could count on his favorite boy, Pieps, to beat him up, Auden's preferred form of defilement.

Throughout history, excluding the hellish interval of the Nazi maelstrom, Germany has been tolerant of homosexuals, the word itself invented in 1869 by Karl-Maria Kertbeny and publically defended for the first time in 1867 by the jurist Karl Heinrich Ulrichs in Munich. In 1897 Magnus Hirschfeld founded the first organization in the defense of homosexuality, the Scientific Humanitarian Committee.

Karl Ulrichs quoted Schopenhauer from his *The World as Will and Representation* in which he wrote that homosexuality was in every culture: "It arises in some way from human nature itself." Schopenhauer was in no way infallible because he added: "It occurred in the old as Nature's way of keeping a man from procreating." Ulrichs went on to note, *à propos* of nothing at all, that homosexuals were drawn to Wagner's magnificent, if syrupy operas, the proof being the popularity to our own day of the Festival of Bayreuth with its well-heeled and well-dressed gays.

In 1885 the Berlin police commissioner Leopold von Meerscheidt-Hüllessem founded the Department of Homosexuals, as reported, to keep track of them for the seemingly benevolent reason of freeing homosexuals from blackmail and the resultant suicides. He personally conducted tours for the rich through the gay dives of the city, where he knew the boys by name, tours that perhaps brought him money from those who were out to do a little slumming because he eventually killed himself when caught accepting bribes from a banker he was protecting from accusations of rape.

It was largely thanks to Meerscheidt-Hüllessem's *laissez-faire* attitude that homosexual restaurants, clubs, bars, indoor and outdoor dance halls and costume balls flourished, and homosexual playgrounds alongside rivers, lakes, canals and railways became popular for immediate consumption. Sexual liberation in Berlin was a drawing power, but equally so was the fact that there was something for everyone: cross-dressers, their cheeks rouged and their eyebrows plucked; sadists paid to stomp on the likes of masochistic Auden; virile hustlers who let johns feel their yards through their trousers, often of military fabrication as soldiers and sailors were well aware of the appeal of their uniforms and positioned themselves just outside their barracks or along the Unter den Linden, in the Tiergarten Park and Friedrichstrasse, known for its prostitutes, and Berlin's Broadway, the Ku' damm. The more one aged, the more one was obliged to exchange the warmth and ambience of clubs and bars in search of johns outside, in parks and along streets, in bath houses and swimming pools.

Magnus Hirschfeld was ostracized by most homosexuals because of his interest in effeminacy, lesbians and cross-dressers, all of which undermined a homosexual man's image of himself as being more virile than straights because homosexuals changed partners more often and had sex more often. This was largely true because men were out for an orgasm, preferably in parks, forests and the like (outdoor sex was always an added stimulant), unions that could rapidly increase in the number of participants out for the same thrill. There was no convincing as was a necessity with women, although heterosexuals maintained that such rites boosted one's lust, while homosexuals knew that what really excited were a few minutes with an unknown male, discovering the mysterious contents shielded by the buttons of a pair of trousers, in places as dangerously exposed as possible.

For the pleasure of the eyes - 13

QUERELLE DE BREST – JEAN GENET
1947

Querelle de Brest was writer/director Fassbinder's last film, released posthumously after his drug overdose in 1982. Jean Genet's 1947 novel of the same name made Genet popular among every effeminate gay in France, starting with Cocteau, although Genet's thing was virile hustlers.

As hot today as in '47, the book relates the life of thief/murderer/largely-homosexual George Querelle from the ship *Le Vengeur*. His hang out is the Feria bar where his brother is the lover of the owner's wife, Lysiane. The owner allows men to fuck her, but only after rolling dice with him. If he wins, he fucks the men, if he loses, they fuck Lysiane. Querelle says he wants the woman but deliberately loses to the owner because it's he that Querelle really hungers for. Querelle's relationship with his brother, Robert, is tight, probably from an intimate boyhood, and soon they're both fucking Lysiane.

From here on what takes place becomes downright raunchy: Querelle kills a man, Vic, over opium. He wants to blame the murder on a construction worker Gil because Gil is being chased by the police for killing his lover Theo. Querelle's brother Robert is in love with Gil and wants Querelle to hide him. Querelle meets Gil and falls in love with him because he resembles his brother Robert, which doesn't stop him from turning Gil over to the police--after they've fucked--so Gil will take the fall for the murder of Vic. The chief of police arrests Gil after, first, meeting Querelle and, second, being fucked by same.

At the end Querelle returns to his ship *Le Vengeur* where the captain has always been in love with him. He knows Querelle murdered Vic, wants to protect him, so he and Querelle ... well ... you know.

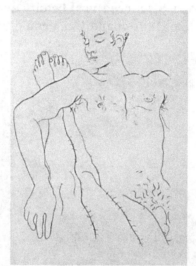

Cocteau's *Querelle* for the pleasure of the eyes - 14

Brad Davis was a physically and sexually abused child, by both parents, who earned a living, when young, as a rent boy in N.Y. called Bobby. He was an alcoholic and took drugs intravenously, starred in Genet's *Querelle* (as a gay sailor in a Fassbinder film) and *Midnight Express*, giving a role of such intensity that I've personally only been able to watch it once, even though it's in my collection of films. He also starred in Joe Orton's play "Entertaining Mr. Sloane", Orton who had his head and face stove in by his boyfriend through jealousy of Orton's successes, who then killed himself. Both men were addicted to rent boys, especially lads in Morocco who would fuck them silly. Brad Davis had a son, Alex, a transsexual born a girl. He kept his last illness a secret so as to continue working to maintain his family, although he was also certainly an extremely private person. He died at age 41.

Brad Davis

A riveting presence, a supernatural beauty and an icon of masculinity, he was the man guys like Hudson and Dean could only dream of becoming.

Jean Genet

Jean Genet (1910 – 1986) was the son of a prostitute and a prostitute himself, as well as a thief, vagabond and all-around small-time hoodlum. His adopted parents, a carpenter and his wife, seemed to have taken loving care of the boy, abandoned at age 7 months, and after their deaths he was taken in by a couple who were unable to stop him from making money with his body, often leaving the house wearing makeup. At age 15 he was failed for three years for misdemeanors and then joined the Foreign Legion at age 18, given a dishonorable discharge for homosexuality. When imprisoned again in 1919 Jean Cocteau, Picasso, Sartre and others got the French president to pardon him. He became chic, the bourgeois' favorite dinner guest, milking his renown for what it was worth, noting along the way that the more he spit in the soup the more French intellectuals praised his difference, the French being traditionally torn between individualism and their adhesion to strictly codified tradition. A voracious reader from early youth, by then he had written five novels and three plays. He contemplated suicide in 1964 when his lover killed himself, but went on to take part in the student revolts of May '68, was invited to N.Y. by the Black Panthers in 1970 (where he met, naturally, Ginsberg and Burroughs), supported the Baader and Meinhof gang, was in Beirut during the Sabra and Shatila massacres in 1982 and spent six months in Palestinian refugee camps, writing various articles in their support. He died in a Paris hotel room in 1986, perhaps from a fall linked to his weakness because of throat cancer diagnosed in 1979. He was buried in Morocco, home of the lover who had chosen death over life.

For the pleasure of the eyes by Charles Demuth - 15

BILLY BUDD
THE OPERA - 1951

Billy Budd was discovered among Herman Melville's papers by his biographer Raymond Weaven. The unfinished manuscript was put together by Harris Hayford and Merton Sealts, which took an astounding 9 years, and was published in 1962. Terence Stamp received an Oscar nomination for his role as Billy in Peter Ustinov's 1962 film adaptation.

Robert Ryan, Terence Stamp and Peter Ustinov.

Melville married, as did a majority of homosexuals during the sexually repressive Victorian Era (repressive but, on the other hand, there were never so many boy/girl whorehouses in London) and Melville was said to have been sexually inhibited himself, although one would have thought the same of Roger Casement and Maynard Keynes had they not left behind diaries in which they described their homosexuality in detail, down to the nature of the acts and the cock sizes of the boys.

Melville's immense luck was Benjamin Britten's decision to use the novella as a basis for his 1951 opera of the same name, whose libretto was written by E.M. Forster and Eric Croizer. Forster and Britten lived part of their lives together, and both associated with the Bloomsbury Set, the description of which will soon follow, the aim being to give an insider's view of the incredible extent of sexual lubricity that was going on in the upper classes, a counterweight to the sexual repression known to the middle and lower classes, although many lower-class boys were both cannon fodder and sexual rent.

On entering the *Indomitable* where he's been shanghaied, Billy sings a stirring goodbye to his former ship, the *Rights-of-Man*, which will eventually give Claggart, the Master-at-Arms, reason to rid himself of Billy who represents purity and beauty, and whom Claggart knows he will never possess. He therefore vows to destroy the boy for awakening his forbidden desires, singing "O beautiful, o handsomeness, goodness!/ Would that I had never seen you! Having seen you what choice remains to me?/None, none! I'm doomed to annihilate you."

While the captain of the ship, Vere, has a more intellectual way of sublimating his want for Billy, referring to the boy as the biblical pearl of great price, meaning that to enter him would equal entry into the Kingdom of Heaven, all the while declaring his intellectual superiority to such thoughts: "I have studied and pondered and tried to fathom eternal truth." He even underlines his inherent goodness to the men, singing "We owe so much to them!'' (I can hear Britten and Forester giggling together when they wrote that.) Most probably Claggart had tried to have his way with Billy who may not have understood his intentions, and it is possible too that Vere tried nothing at all.

Claggart's unrequited love for the lad led him to accuse Billy of inciting a mutiny, an accusation so monstrous that the boy--whose physical impediment, a stutter, inhibited from defending himself--had no alternative to striking out at Claggart, who died (the role in the film was played by Robert Ryan, a man so unwholesome in aspect that one could only applaud his demise). Vere orders a court-marshal and Billy is sentenced to death, which draws this outburst from Vere: ''Struck dead by the angel of God! Yet the angel must hang!'' Billy forgives him in another stirring area, ''God bless Captain Vere!''. Billy's hanging moves the crew to near desperate revolt, of enormous choral beauty.

Vere is of course accused, today, of removing sexual temptation by his destruction of Billy, but although the crew nearly mutinied it is known that during those times Vere had had no choice other than taking the action he did, if he wanted to sustain his control over the ship thereafter.

Rictor Norton in an excellent article mentions that the ship's surgeon failed to understand why there was no muscular spasm (Melville wrote that there had been none), and wonders if Melville's readers understand that the surgeon is talking about the orgasm and ejaculation that at times occur when a man is hanged, one reason, Norton points out, that reformers felt that hangings were obscene.

I would like to turn now to the sexuality of the times, as represented by the Bloomsbury Set, which both Forster and Britten were part of.

Rainer Werner Fassbinder's last and most controversial film.

It was created by a man who thrived on controversy.

It will take you into a surreal world of passion and sexuality.

It's a film that goes further than most would dare to go.

This is Querelle.

This is Fassbinder's final statement.

Querelle

Based upon the novel by Jean Genet

DIETER SCHIDOR and GAUMONT present
BRAD DAVIS · FRANCO NERO ·
JEANNE MOREAU · LAURENT MALET
in QUERELLE
A film by RAINER WERNER FASSBINDER
Based on the novel by JEAN GENET "QUERELLE DE BREST"
A TRIUMPH FILMS RELEASE, a PLANET FILM, MUNICH - GAUMONT, PARIS · MCMLXXXII All rights reserved.

For the pleasure of the eyes – 16

SAILORS IN HOLLYWOOD
CA. 1950

Henry Willson was Hollywood's chief agent in the 1950s, agent being a synonym for pimp and/or casting couch. He was called "pure evil" by some, "slime that oozed from under a rock" by another. He searched everywhere for boys to represent: Alan Delon was found dancing in a Cannes disco, Tab Hunter at an ice rink, and Rock Hudson sent out pictures of himself to every agent in Hollywood, and only Willson replied. Hudson arrived in Hollywood fresh from the Great Lakes Naval Training Station, home of the Navy boot camp. Willson taught his boys how to eat and how to walk, he saw to it that they got lessons in acting, new teeth, tailored clothing, and he got a percentage *and* the sex his boys gave him in exchange. He pimped out the boys and girls in exchange for money and/or favors. He's said to have worshipped Rock Hudson, actually promising him that one day he would be received in the White House, which was the case, while the wealthy Willson ended up in a pauper's grave.

Part of Willson's job was to smother scandals, and he did it so well his boys could participate in pool orgies without fear of discovery, unless it was Willson himself who turned them in. He went so far as to marry his secretary to one of them when the press came close to discovering the actor was gay.

Henry was nonetheless close to actors in more than sex. He befriended them, listened to their stories, gave advice, tons of advice; he protected them and even fathered them. He was known to be honest with his boys: if he slept with one, the lad was assured of getting a role in a film.

Willson himself related the story of Rory Calhoun and Guy Madison. Rory was an ex-convict who had began by stealing groceries before working up to jewels and cars. When caught, he was sent to San Quentin, at age 18. Out riding on a horse through the hills above Hollywood after his release, Rory came on a woman who liked his looks and told him she knew an agent that might be interested in representing him. When Henry got to known Rory better he deemed the boy too huge to be accommodated by most men, and anyway Rory had no interest in that kind of sex, preferring women when not obliged to sleep with Willson. Guy Madison was also a client of Henry's who had refused intercourse with him because it was not his thing. Then, on a certain rainy day, Willson, lonely, decided to drive out to see Rory. In front of Rory's home Willson recognized the Jaguar belonging to Guy. As he approached the Jag he could see it was wildly rocking. Drawing closer, he saw Calhoun fucking Guy, seemingly impossible because Guy had assured him that he was virgin (in that way) and Henry thought that Rory was simply too big. Later Guy swore that it had been the first time for him, as it had been for Rory (Rory said, although he had spent years in prison when he was a boy, and everyone knows what that means).

Later, when reporters were getting too close to Hudson, who was bringing in a fortune for Willson, some believe Willson turned over documents to the press exposing Rory's imprisonment, in order to get them interested elsewhere. For weeks afterwards Rory was constantly in the news.

Tab Hunter was a kid raised by a single mom. He went to a military academy, was a soda jerk, an usher, and at age 15 he entered the Coast Guard by lying about his age. At 12 he had worked at a riding academy where he met an actor. On furloughs from the Coast Guard he crashed at the actor's apartment. No one knows at what age their affaire began. The actor put the boy on to Willson whose attempts at seduction Hunter *said* he had successfully avoided. But Hunter was later rounded up with 26 other naked guys at a gay pool party, that became known as Tab's Pajama Game when exposed by *Confidential* magazine, which had a circulation of 4 million. Tab was obliged to switch to television, but in 2007 he was added to the Hollywood Walk of Fame.

Omnisexual Brando often played the sailor and advised a boy to
always go in the direction his erect dick pointed: it *never*
makes a mistake.

THE ROYAL NAVY'S MACINTYRE REPORT OF 1968

Sir John Bush, Admiral of the Western Fleet, ordered the MacIntyre Report that comforted him in his belief that there wasn't a single royal ship where homosexual practices were unknown.

Two major ports were outstanding in the number of homosexual acts that took place, the first in Singapore were the boys were visiting male prostitutes who were dressed as girls, girls, admitted the report, who smelled "delicious", but, as one commander underlined, even if some of the rent-boys were gorgeous, sailors could not have chosen to return a second time once they'd found out the truth of their gender after a first visit-- although most did, prompting the navy to discharge 300 of them.

The second citadel of vice was the Bahamas where the boys got free liquor in exchange for posing for pornographic photos, which made the pornographers a fortune. In pre-W.W. II Berlin thousands of books could be bought at kiosks showing boys nude (the cock long but always more or less soft). Afterwards a lead curtain descended over pornography, so if a lad wanted to see a cunt, for example, he had to be invited into the backroom of special shops where he fingered through shoeboxes of photos until finding one that turned him on. (I know, because as a very young boy I visited such sites in London with a very horny young heterosexual friend of mine). Photos showing naked, erect sailors were rare and far more expensive. It's not because everything goes in the Internet Age today that there wasn't a time when a lad would beat off after getting an eyeful of a girl's inadvertently uncovered ankle.

The catalyst for ordering the report was, apparently, the belief that sailors could be blackmailed into giving up military secrets, and so had to be sternly lectured on keeping their hands to themselves. The MacIntyre Report maintained, interestingly, that *most males* had homosexual tendencies, but that 95% of them grew out of it by age 22. The high number of boys who did other boys was due to British boarding schools, where the lads were actually fucking each other nightly (6). Churchill later said that the tradition of the Royal Navy was ''rum, sodomy and the lash''. One can only wonder what he did at his prep school, Harrow, because as a youth he was good-looking in the extreme, and as one soldier wrote when Churchill wandered over to piss side-by-side with him during W.W. II, ''He's hung like a horse''.

Churchill – For the pleasure of the eyes - 17

THE *USS IOWA* DISASTER OF 1989

The accusations behind the cause of the explosion on the *USS Iowa* in 1989, and the botched investigation that followed, are so disgusting and heartbreaking that I'm not going to prolong the misery by repeating the name of the man accused of murdering 47 youths, youths who still had the near entirety of their lives before them, as well as the destruction of 47 families, and the very desire to continue on for those who lost a son.

On the 19 of April Turret Two's central gun blew up within the confines of the turret compartment, a tragedy that hundreds of other sailors escaped thanks to the turret's blast doors. The resulting fire took 90 minutes to put out and the turret's magazine was flooded with seawater to prevent further explosions.

Clay Heart (a pseudonym) was blamed for setting off the conflagration due to an electrical or chemical detonator, the aim being to commit suicide due to a homosexual love interest that had gone sour with his lover Kent True (a pseudonym), all the while leaving True $100,000, the exclusive beneficiary of Heart's insurance policy.

True's wife was interrogated to find out what kind of lover her husband was, the frequency of their rapports, the nature of their sex and if she'd accommodated any of True's buddies.

Heart's best friend, Mike Smith (a pseudonym), was questioned for nearly 8 hours by NIS (Naval Investigative Service) agents who told him that if he didn't admit that Heart blew up Turret Two he would be accused of murder, perjury and obstruction of justice. Smith was allowed to return to duty on the *Iowa* where he immediately began a 9-hour watch, after which he was immediately interrogated by the NIS for an additional 6 hours until he admitted that Heart had not only sexually propositioned him, but had shown him the device he was planning to us to blow up the turret, a confession he later retracted.

Traces of the detonating device were found by the Navy laboratory at Norfolk, but a later FBI laboratory found that the traces were due to the explosion itself. Extremely damaging was the report that both Heart and True had been interrogated *before* the explosion concerning their being a gay couple. Alas, we know nothing more, except that the matter was dropped.

Lastly, in Heart's locker two damning books were found, one entitled *Getting Even: The Complete Book of Dirty Tricks*, wherein there was a guide on how to build bombs, and *Improved Munitions Handbook*, that gave instructions on how to build bombs and detonators.

The television magazine *60 Minutes* questioned the Navy's accusations, while the newspaper the *Washington Post* supported the accusations. That both medias are American glories does not exclude possible errors in their reports and conclusions.

In Heart's favor we have the incredibly damning report that officers on the *Iowa*, behind the ship captain's back, decided to try out a new supercharged powder that crew members deemed was too strong for the old turrets, lamenting that their lives were in danger. And as a matter of fact the *Iowa* was indeed old, having served in W.W. II and Korea, and had been mothballed until Reagan had it refurbished. Although millions were spent on the ship, mechanical problems of every imaginable sort remained-- even the sprinklers, following the explosion, didn't go off. Older crewmen knew the new "kids" had not received enough training, and explained that they were understaffed. When one of the gunners brought all this out in an interrogation he was halted by an officer who cried out, "You little shit! You can't say that!" His remarks were expunged.

An independent commission was brought in in 1991 and, after spending $25 million on the investigation, the verdict was that there was "no plausible accident" explanation for the explosion, and "no intentional" explanation either. The Navy apologized to Heart's family and the *Iowa* was decommissioned in 1990. In 1991, during the Gulf War, two *Iowa*-class battleships fired 1,182 rounds from guns identical to that which had exploded, without mishap (although it is doubtful they used the incriminated "supercharged" powder).

A warship firing its guns.

ANY MOTHER'S SON
1969 - 1992

Allen Schindler was murdered at age 23 for being gay, something he apparently didn't hide as slightly before his death he had wired, throughout the Pacific, an announcement on secure navy lines "2-Q-T-2-B-S-T-R-8" (too cute to be straight). He was restricted to his ship, the *USS Belleau Wood*, but allowed shore leave four days before his assassination.

He was stomped to death in a park, his penis severed, so disfigured he was identified by his family only thanks to his tattoo. The scum found guilty of the murder had been witnessed singing throughout the entire beating. He escaped death by pleading guilty and said he regretted nothing, adding he would have done it again. Sentenced to life in a military facility, his case can nonetheless be reevaluated, under military law, every year.

A prize-winning film, *Any Mother's Son*, recounts his ordeal.

For the pleasure of the eyes - 18

A NAVY SEAL – 2003

The Navy SEALS (Sea, Air and Land Teams) became world famous when they killed Bin Laden, and may be the world's number one intervention force, although the Israelis can't be far behind, if they are behind.

The story of Brett Jones is heartrending because he was a SEAL who accidently outed himself by leaving an I-love-you phone message to his sailor lover. He left the Navy in 2003, after having been thrown out of his home by his Air Force pilot father and mother when he was an adolescent, due to his homosexuality.

He married a former detective and inherited the detective's 13-year-old son, all three forming a seamless bond. They decided to settle down in Alabama where they were treated like lepers, their son even passed messages in school with Bible verses concerning his two dads' sins.

Brett's close SEAL buddies supported him but not the corps, and a Navy investigation into his sexuality ended only thanks to the intervention of equal-rights lawyers and several congressmen.

Jones and White married in Indiana in 2011, White's dad embracing his boy. White's son, straight, is now becoming a pilot. He calls White Dad and Jones Brett. As Brett worked in security in Afghanistan and Iraq, and White was a cop, they opened a security company. The company, and their new lives, are a success.

Brett, Brett and Brett on the far right, for the pleasure of the eyes - 19

DON'T ASK / DON'T TELL

I'd like to broach the late 1900s with the lives of two sailors Steven Zeeland brings to our attention is his *Sailors and Sexual Identity*, 1995.

The stories come in the midst of President Clinton's Don't Ask, Don't Tell law, universally known as DADT, instituted in 1994 (the law was later extended to Don't Pursue and still later Don't Harass). The law simply relaxed restrictions on gays, who could nonetheless be prosecuted if they *did* tell or if they were caught doing it on ships. Rescinded in 2011, today's gays are apparently accepted in the armed forces, with the exceptions of transsexuals. Engaging in homosexual acts on navy property has been a no-no since 1776, since the American Revolution, and during W.W. II only ''normal'' boys were allowed through screening, which homosexuals clearly were not. During said screening I personally admitted to my preference for boys, although I was still years away from touching someone ''in that way''. As a Mormon, lads my age didn't touch girls until marriage, and the subject of boys doing boys was so outlandish that it never came up in seminary classes, although the hellfire awaiting those who jerked-off was gone over tirelessly (the dire consequences of which were explained to us by some hellishly handsome young seminary teachers who were certainly lying through their teeth when they claimed to be innocent of such perversion). So I escaped the infernal of Vietnam, but became an exile, leaving gruesome Utah for Paris, never to step foot in my native country again (7).

One of the surprising endorsers of the original DADT law was the senator and former Major General Barry Goldwater, who stated that ''you don't have to be straight to shoot straight'' (had I known that before, I would have detested him far less).

A poll taken in 2006 by Zogby International found that among military men who knew that homosexuals were among them, 27% were against their presence, saying it had a negative impact on morale, 64% said it had no impact and 3% a positive impact.

During the years of DADT 13,650 men were discharged for not respecting sexual anonymity (from W.W. II to the end of DADT 114,000 men were discharged for homosexual activity of some sort).

Back to Zeeland's two sailors, one, Antony, 23, and Eddie, 22. Both had had atrocious childhoods, in one case losing parents to drugs, in another through an automobile accident, both sexually abused during their youths, one hating it, the other hoping for more. Both had had sex with girls but preferred the virility and lust inherent in boys. Both had met on the *USS Ranger*. Antony felt that men were dogs; Eddie liked everyone and was liked by everyone, even those who knew about his sexuality.

Antony prided himself on being a father figure to Eddie and was into Marines as not only being the best sex, but assuring Zeeland that you've never made love until you've had a Marine. His best experience was with four Marines, starting out in a whirlpool with kissing and groping, and ending up with all four begging Antony to fuck them. With time the sex became more and more violent, and the supply of boys was so unending that Antony was soon sated. Byron had written the same thing to a friend when he'd fucked 200 boys on an excursion to Athens (*Le Grand Tour* necessary to the education of every British boy[6]), promising he would never fuck again.

My own experience with the American military took place when I visited friends in Stuttgart, one of whom I'd made wondrous love to on a beach in Myconos, although he now had someone else. We went to a club frequented by navy and army boys and when I returned from a ten-minute break in the john I found seven beers on my table (something unthinkable in French culture). The waiter pointed out the boys who had offered them, all army and sailor guys, one of whom was exactly the kind that turned me on, smaller than me, in jeans, black hair and eyes, and the face of a fallen angel. Back to my friend's apartment the sailor and I literally fucked the night away, a marathon I'd never known before nor since. This was the kind of sex Antony sought, the kind provided by Marines.

Antony was Eddy's best friend, although sexually Eddy was tame--the kissing and caressing type. They had met on the *USS Ranger* where Antony took advantage of every nook to have sex, while Eddy was too afraid of being found out. Eddy said there were plenty of places to play around on the ship, the fantail of which was so black you could only feel what you were doing, although Eddy refused to go there. Eddy hated Marines, finding them stuck on themselves and behaving as if they could walk on water. He had sex with Marines only when he was drunk and they sufficiently pleaded.

Eddy thought that homosexuals were less promiscuous than heteros, giving his roommate as an example, a boy who had a different girl every night, on the bed next to Eddy's, while Eddy put on earphones to drown out the girls' screams. He said straights screwed anything with a vagina, while gays were choosy. Although I personally believe gays are far more promiscuous than heterosexuals, I know too that they're more difficult in their choices, always going for the best-looking boys. The proof of this is the book *Full Service* by Scotty Bowers, a 150-hour interview taped and put in book form by Lionel Frieberg. It's a miracle because Bowers decided to tape his tell-all in 2012 when he was 88. Bowers opened a gas station just after W.W. II and because he was a good-looking ex-Marine, always willing to turn an extra buck in the American tradition, he offered himself for rent, and as his clientele increased he hired Marine friends to care for the needs of Hollywood actors, producers, et al., Marines who serviced guys and/or gals, and later women to service guys and other women.

Bower's Marines often had a great time, were served great food around great pools, and did what his clients wanted, which was often just a human presence and a little mutual jerking off. Some of the boys wound up living with the men, as found in the scene from *Some Like It Hot* where Jack Lemmon returns from his date with Osgood and declares to Tony Curtis that he and Osgood were going to get married. "Why would a guy marry another guy?" asked Curtis. "For *security*!" exclaimed Lemmon.

Bowers and his Marines were easy-going guys, and having fun with them must have been fun in itself. I've recovered photos showing some of the Marines employed by Scotty at his gas station. They looked like nice, pleasant fellows that it would have been a pleasure to have had a beer with … and maybe more. I'm glad Scotty Bowers existed, and lived long enough to tell his tale. I'm glad his memory remained so intact and that a publisher dared print a book that includes such men as Tracy, Clift, Perkins, Hughes, Flynn and dozens of others. I wish I could find someone like Scotty and his pals who would ease *my* later years!

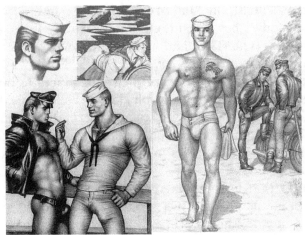

For the pleasure of the eyes - 20

TODAY

Nearly all gay sailors are cautious with whom they discus their sexual orientation. The problem is that once a man is outed, he's outed for good. The Navy SEAL whose homosexuality became known seems to have been fully accepted by those who knew him, but not by the vast number of SEALs who did not know him personally, a contempt which forced him to leave (a contempt that has led, in other cases, to suicide). A sailor working in a small unite may well feel justified in outing himself, and may well be accepted by the majority of his colleagues. But what happens when he is then posted to a bigger base, where he will never know everyone personally, but where he will soon be known as the post queer?

So the average sailor will continue to either hide his sexuality or pretend to be heterosexual (or at the very least avoid the subject). The times in which we live are as homosexually open as any since the early Greeks and Romans. Yet a boy would nonetheless be crazy to admit to his locker-room buddies that he prefers them to the maidens in the showers next door, and this will not change for a long, long time, if ever.

The vast majority of gays adopt a wait-and-see attitude, which they should, revealing the truth to a select number of acquaintances. The social isolation is difficult to live with, the stress a burden, especially as boys have known from childhood the names reserved for queers. Zero homophobic intolerance can be imposed on a crew, but who would want to live with being just tolerated? It would seem logical that under such conditions a gay's competence in what he does would be adversely affected, yet ship commanders maintain that homosexuals fulfill their duties, at the very least, as competently as straights.

For the pleasure of the eyes today - 21

SOURCES

(1) See my book *TROY*.
(2) See my book *Gay Genius*.
(3) See my book *Greek Homosexuality*.
(4) See my book *Buckingham*.
(5) See my book *Homosexual Warriors*.
(6) See my book *Homosexual Boarding Schools*.
(7) See my book *Michael Hone*.

Abbott Jacob, *History of Pyrrhus*, 2009.
Ady, Cecilia, *A History of Milan under the Sforza*, 1907.
Aldrich, Robert, *Who's Who in Gay and Lesbian History*, 2001.
Apollonius of Rhodes, *Argonautica*, 3rd century B.C.
Aristophanes, Bantam Drama, 1962.
Aronson, Marc, *Sir Walter Ralegh*, 2000.
Baglione, *Caravaggio*, circa 1600.
Baker Simon, *Ancient Rome*, 2006.
Barber, Richard, *The Devil's Crown--Henry II and Sons*, 1978.
Barber, Stanley, *Alexandros*, 2010.
Beachy, Robert, *Gay Berlin*, 2014. Marvelous.
Bellori, *Caravaggio*, circa 1600.
Bergreen, Laurence, *Over the Edge of the World. Magellan.* 2003.
Bicheno, Hugh, *Vendetta,* 2007.
Bierman, John, *Dark Safari, Henry Morton Stanley*, 1990.

Blanchard, Jean-Vincent, *Éminence, Cardinal Richelieu and the Rise of*
Boyd, Douglas, *April Queen*, 2004.
Boyles, David, *Blondel's Song*, 2005.
Bramly, Serge, *Leonardo*, 1988. A wonderful book.
Burg, B.R., *Gay Warriors*, 2002.
Burg, B.R., *Sodomy and the Pirate Tradition*, 1989.
Bury and Meiggs, *A History of Greece*, 1975.
Calimach, Andrew, *Lover's Legends*, 2002.
Carroll, Stuart, *Maryrs & Murderers, The Guise Family*, 2009.
Carry Peter, *True History of the Kelly Gang*, 2000.
Cawthorne, Nigel, *Sex Lives of the Popes*, 1996.
Cellini, Benvenuto, *The Autobiography of Benvenuto Cellini.*
Ceram, C.W., *Gods, Graves and Scholars*, 1951.
Chamberlin, E.R. *The Fall of the House of Borgia*, 1974.
Cloulas, Ivan, *The Borgia*, 1989.
Cooper, John, *The Queen's Agent*, 2011.
Crompton, Louis, *Byron and Greek Love*, 1985.
Crompton, Louis, *Homosexuality and Civilization*, 2003.
Crouch, David, *William Marshal*, 1990.
Crowley, Roger, *Empires of the Sea*, 2008. Marvelous.
Crowley, Roger, *Empires of the Sea*, 2008. Marvelous.
Curtis Cate, *Friedrich Nietzsche*, 2002.
Dale, Richard, *Who Killed Sir Walter Ralegh?*, 2011.
Davidson, James, *Courtesans and Fishcakes*, 1998.
Davidson, James, *The Greeks and Greek Love*, 2007.
Davis, John Paul, *The Gothic King, Henry III*, 2013.
Defored, Frank, *Big Bill Tilden*, 1975.
Dover K.J. *Greek Homosexuality*, 1978
Duby, George, *William Marshal*, 1985.
Eisler, Benita, *BYRON Child of Passion, Fool of Fame*, 2000. Wonderful.
Erlanger, Philippe, *The King's Minion*, 1901.
Everitt Anthony, *Augustus*, 2006.
Everitt Anthony, *Cicero*, 2001.
Everitt, Anthony, *Hadrian*, 2009.
Fagles, Robert, *The Iliad*, 1990.
Forellino, Antonio, *Michelangelo*, 2005. Beautiful reproductions.
Frieda, Leonie, *Catherine de Medici*, 2003. Wonderful.
Gayford, Martin, *Michelangelo*, 2013. A beautiful book.
Gillingham, John, *Richard the Lionheart*, 1978.
Goldsworthy Adrian, *Caesar*, 2006
Goldsworthy Adrian, *The Fall of Carthage*, 2000.
Goodman Rob and Soni Jimmy, *Rome's Last Citizen*, 2012.
Goodwin, Robert, *SPAIN*, 2015.

Graham-Dixon, Andrew, *Caravaggio* 2010. Fabulous.

Grant Michael, *History of Rome*, 1978.

Graves, Robert, *Greek Myths*, 1955.

Grazia, Sebastian de, *Machiavelli in Hell*, 1989.

Guicciardini, *Storie fiorentine (History of Florence)*, 1509. Essential.

Halperin David M. *One Hundred Years of Homosexuality*, 1990.

Harris Robert, *Imperium*, 2006.

Herodotus, *The Histories*, Penguin Classics.

Hesiod and Theognis, Penguin Classics, 1973.

Hibbert, Christopher, *Florence, the Biography of a City*, 1993.

Hibbert, Christopher, *The Borgias and Their Enemies*, 2009.

Hibbert, Christopher, *The Great Mutiny India 1857*, 1978. Fabulous.

Hibbert, Christopher, *The Rise and Fall of the House of Medici*, 1974.

Hicks, Michael, *Richard III*, 2000.

Hine, Daryl, *Puerilities*, 2001.

Hochschild, Adam, *King Leopold's Ghost*, 1999.

Holland Tom, *Rubicon*, 2003.

Hughes Robert, *Rome*, 2011.

Hughes-Hallett, *Heroes*, 2004.

Hughes, Robert, *Rome*, 2011.

Hughes, Robert, *The Fatal Shore*, 1987.

Hulot, Frédéric, *Suffren, l'Amiral Satan*, 1994.

Hutchinson, Robert, *Elizabeth's Spy Master*, 2006.

Hutchinson, Robert, *House of Treason*, 2009.

Hutchinson, Robert, *Thomas Cromwell*, 2007.

Jack Belinda, *Beatrice's Spell*, 2004.

Jeal, Tim, *Explorers of the Nile*, 2011. Wonderful.

Jeal, Tim, *STANLEY*, 2007. All of Jeal's books are must-reads.

Johnson, Marion, *The Borgias*, 1981.

Köhler, Joachim, *Zarathustra's Secret*, 1989.

Korda, Michael, *HERO The Life and Legend of Lawrence of Arabia*, 2010.

Lacey, Robert, *Henry VIII*, 1972.

Lacy, Robert, *Sir Walter Ralegh*, 1973.

Lambert, Gilles *Caravaggio*, 2007.

Landucci, Luca, *A Florentine Diary*, around 1500, a vital source.

Lev, Elizabeth, *The Tigress of Forli*, 2011. Wonderfully written.

Levy, Buddy, *Conquistador*, 2009.

Levy, Buddy, *River of Darkness*, 2011. Fabulous.

Lévy, *Edmond, Sparte, 1979.*

Lewis, Bernard, *The Assassins*, 1967.

Livy, *Rome and the Mediterranean*

Livy, *The War with Hannibal.*

Lubkin, Gregory, *A Renaissance Court*, 1994.

Lyons, Mathew, *The Favourite*, 2011.

Macintyre, Ben, *The Man Who Would Be King*, 2004.

Mackay, James, *In My End is My Beginning, Mary Queen of Scots*, 1999.

Mallett, Michael and Christine Shaw, *The Italian Wars 1494-1559*.

Malye, Jean, *La Véritable Histore d'Alcibiade*, 2009.

Manchester, William, *A World Lit Only By Fire*, 1993.

Mancini, *Caravaggio*, circa 1600.

Marchand, Leslie, *Byron*, 1971.

Martines, Lauro, *April Blood-Florence and the Plot against the Medici*, 2003.

Matyszak, Philip, *The Mithridates the Great*, 2008.

McLynn, Frank, *Richard and John, Kings of War*, 2007. Fabulous.

McLynn, *Marcus Aurelius*, 2009.

McLynn, *STANLEY, The making of an African explorer*, 1989.

Meier, Christian, *Caesar*, 1996.

Meyer, G.J. *The Borgias, The Hidden History*, 2013.

Meyer, G.J. *The Tudors*, 2010.

Meyer, Jack, *Alcibiades*, 2009.

Miles Richard, *Ancient Worlds*, 2010.

Miles Richard, *Carthage Must be Destroyed*, 2010.

Miller, David, *Richard the Lionheart*, 2003.

Moore Lucy, *Amphibious Thing*, 2000.

Moote, Lloyd, *Louis XIII, The Just*, 1989.

Mortimer, Ian, 1415, *Henry V's Year of Glory*, 2009.

Nicholl, Charles, *The Reckoning*, 2002.

Noel, Gerard, *The Renaissance Popes*, 2006.

Noel, Gerard, *The Renaissance Popes*, 2006.

Opper Thorsten, *Hadrian*, 2008.

Opper, Thorsten, *Hadrian, Empire and Conflict*, 2008.

Parker, Derek, *Cellini*, 2003, the book is beautifully written.

Pascal, Jean Claude, *L'Amant du Roi*, 1991.

Payne, Robert and Nihita Romanoff, *Ivan the Terrible*, 2002.

Pernot, Michel, *Henri III*, Le Roi Décrié, 2013, Excellent book.

Petitfils, Jean-Christian, *Louis XIII*, 2008, wonderful.

Peyrefitte, Roger, *Alexandre*, 1979.

Plutarch's Lives, Modern Library.

Pollard, .J., *Warwick the Kingmaker*, 2007.

Polybius, *The Histories*.

Read, Piers Paul, *The Templars*, 1999.

Reid, B.L., *The Lives of Roger Casement*, 1976.

Renucci Pierre, *Caligula*, 2000.

Reston, James, *Warriors of God, Richard and the Crusades*, 2001.

Rice, Edward, *Captain Sir Richard Francis Burton*, 1990.

Ridley, Jasper, *The Tudor Age*, 1998.

Robb, Peter, M – *The Man Who Became Caravaggio*, 1998.

Robb, Peter, *Street Fight in Naples*, 2010.

Rocco, Antonio, *Alcibiade Enfant à l'Ecole*, 1630.

Rocke, Michael, *Forbidden Friendships*, 1996. Fabulous/indispensible.

Romans Grecs et Latin, Gallimard, 1958.

Ross, Charles, *Richard III*, 1981.

Rouse, W.H.D., Homer's *The Iliad*, 1938.

Royle, Trevor, *Fighting Mac, The Downfall of Sir Hector Macdonald*.

Ruggiero, Guido, *The Boundaries of Eros*, 1985.

Sabatini, Rafael, *The Life of Cesare Borgia*, 1920.

Saint Bris, Gonzague, *Henri IV*, 2009.

Saslow, James, *Ganymede in the Renaissance*, 1986.

Schiff, Stacy, *Cleopatra*, 2010.

Seward, Desmond, *Caravaggio – A Passionate Life*, 1998.

Simonetta, Marcello, *The Montefeltro Conspiracy*, 2008. Wonderful.

Skidmore, Chris, *Death and the Virgin*, 2010.

Skidmore, *Death and the Virgin*, 2007.

Solnon, Jean-Fançois, *Henry III*, 1996.

Stewart, Alan, *The Cradle King, A Life of James VI & I*, 2003.

Stewart, Alan, *The Cradle King, A Life of James VI & I*, 2003.

Stirling, Stuart, *Pizarro Conqueror of the Inca*, 2005.

Strathern, Paul, *The Medici, Godfathers of the Renaissance*, 2003. Superb.

Strauss Barry, *The Spartacus War*, 2009.

Stuart, Stirling, *Pizarro - Conqueror of the Inca*, 2005.

Suetonius, *The Twelve Caesars*

Tacitus, *The Annals of Imperial Rome.*

Tacitus, *The Histories.*

Thucydides, *The Peloponnesian War,* Penguin Classics.

Tibullus, *The Elegies of Tibullus*, translated by Theodore C. Williams

Turner, Ralph, *Eleanor of Aquitaine*, 2009.

Unger Miles, *Magnifico, The Brilliant Life and Violent Times*

Unger, Miles, *Machiavelli*, 2008.

Vasari, We would know next to nothing if it were not for him.

Vernant, Jean-Pierre, *Mortals and Immortals*, 1991.

Virgil, *The Aeneid*, Everyman's Library, Knopf, 1907.

Viroli, Maurizio, *Niccolo's Smile, A Biography of Machiavelli*, 1998.

Ward-Perkins Bryan, *The Fall of Rome*, 2005

Warren, W.L., *Henry II*, 1973.

Weir, Alison, *Eleanor of Aquitaine*, 1999. Weir is a fabulous writer.

Weir, Alison, *Mary, Queen of Scots*, 2003.

Weir, Alison, *The Wars of the Roses*, 1995.

Wheaton James, *Spartacus*, 2011.

Wikipedia: Research today is impossible without the aid of this monument.

Williams Craig A. *Roman Homosexuality*, 2010.
Williams John, *Augustus*, 1972.
Wilson, Derek, *The Uncrowned Kings of England*, 2005.
Wright, Ed, *History's Greatest Scandals*, 2006.
Wroe, Ann, *Perkin, A Story of Deception*, 2003. Fabulous
Xenophon, *A History of My Times*, Penguin Classics.
Xenophon, *The Persian Expedition*, 1949.
Zeeland, Steven, *Sailors and Sexual Identity*, 1995.

CPSIA information can be obtained
at www.ICGtesting.com
Printed in the USA
BVHW041305300621
610890BV00010B/243